D1008821

Date Due		
5-18-04		

Belongs to:
MPS/Native American Educ Program
1025 N Country Club Dr.
Mesa, AZ 85201

LIBRARY OF AMERICAN
INDIAN HISTORY

UNSUNG HEROES
OF WORLD
WAR II

▲

The Story of the
Navajo Code Talkers

Deanne Durrett

Facts On File, Inc.

TO THE NAVAJO CODE TALKERS

Unsung Heroes of World War II: The Story of the Navajo Code Talkers

Facts On File, Inc.
11 Penn Plaza
New York NY 10001

Library of Congress Cataloging-in-Publication Data
Durrett, Deanne, 1940–
    Unsung Heroes of World War II : the story of the Navajo code talkers / Deanne Durrett.
        p. cm. — (Library of American Indian history)
    Includes bibliographical references and index.
    Summary: Describes the role of a select group of Navajo Marines who developed a code based on their own native language that provided a means for secure communications among American forces in the Pacific during World War II.
    ISBN 0-8160-3603-9
    1. World War, 1939–1945—Cryptography—Juvenile literature. 2. World War, 1939–1945—Participation, Indian—Juvenile literature. 3. Navajo language—Juvenile literature. 4. Navajo Indians—Juvenile literature. 5. United States. Marine Corps—Indian troops—Juvenile literature. [1. World War, 1939–1945—Participation, Indian. 2. United States. Marine Corps—Indian troops. 3. Cryptography. 4. Navajo Indians. 5. Indians of North America—Southwest, New.] I. Title. II. Series.
    D810.C88D87 1998
    940.54'8673—dc21   97-50083

Facts On File books are available at special discounts when purchased in bulk quantities for businesses, associations, institutions or sales promotions. Please call our Special Sales Department in New York at 212/967-8800 or 800/322-8755.

You can find Facts On File on the World Wide Web at http://www.factsonfile.com

Layout by Robert Yaffe
Cover design by Amy Beth Gonzalez
Illustrations on pages 3, 15, 28, 61, and 83 by Patricia Meschino

Printed in the United States of America.

MP FOF 10 9 8 7 6 5 4 3

This book is printed on acid-free paper.

CONTENTS

▲

Preface		iv
Acknowledgments		vi
1:	The Navajo	1
2:	Birth of the Idea	13
3:	The Original 29	25
4:	Special Assignment	36
5:	The Navajo School	48
6:	The Code Talkers Hit Guadalcanal	59
7:	The Navajo Code in Operation	71
8:	The Code Talkers' Shining Hour	82
9:	Home Again	96
10:	The Code Talkers' Contribution	110
Selected Further Reading List		116
Index		119

PREFACE

▲

During World War II, a select group of Navajos were recruited by the U.S. Marines for special service. The first 29 volunteered without knowing what the "special service" would be. When they found out they were to create a code based on their native language they were overwhelmed for several reasons. First, at the boarding schools they had attended, the use of the Navajo language had been forbidden. Second, they didn't have any idea how codes were created. Third, because they were already Marines, sworn to defend the United States and to follow orders, they had no choice but to create a code. Impossible as it seemed the first morning they were given their orders, by "lights out" that night they fell asleep committing the first 26 words in the Navajo Code to memory.

Within weeks, the Navajo Code and the Code Talkers were combat ready. As hoped, the Code Talkers proved themselves on the battlefield, and the Navajo Code completely stymied the Japanese.

From Guadalcanal to Okinawa the Code Talkers were a reliable communication link between U.S. Marines in the field and their commanders. Many among those who fought on the black sand of Iwo Jima say the battle would not have been won without the Navajo Code Talkers. Historians have recorded the importance of the victory on Iwo Jima. Without it, the war in the Pacific would have lasted much longer, more people would have died, and the war's outcome might have been different. The Code Talkers are recognized as vital members of the military team that defeated the Japanese, and the Navajo Code is the only oral combat code that was never broken.

ACKNOWLEDGMENTS

In writing this book I gained a great respect for the Navajo and the Code Talkers. They waited more than 20 years for recognition. Even in civilian life they followed their orders to keep silent in order to protect the security of the code. As I wrote the last line of the last chapter I couldn't help but raise my right hand to my brow in salute to the Navajo Code Talkers. I hope this book will expand the understanding of their contribution to the victory in World War II as well as the importance of preserving the cultures of all people.

I have tried to be accurate in writing about the Code Talkers. Many of the quotes are from the Doris Duke Collection at the University of Utah. I have taken care to record these quotes as they were transcribed by the university. Accounts of the events differ. My research is extensive, and from combined sources I have tried to present an accurate account of happenings.

I wish to express my appreciation to the staff at the Marriott Library at the University of Utah, especially Stan Larson; to the Navajo Tribe and Code Talker Association, the Choctaw Tribe, the U.S. Marine Corps, Barbara Thurber at the Museum of Northern Arizona, R. Rayburn at the National Archives, and numerous others I encountered along the research trail. And, last but certainly not least, to my husband who retired shortly before I began work on this book and is waiting patiently for me to take some time for fun and travel.

THE NAVAJO

A bout 9:00 A.M., February 19, 1945, the first wave of U.S. Marines stormed ashore on the Pacific island of Iwo Jima. They met little Japanese resistance, and many thought the weeks of heavy naval bombardment preceding the landing had brought an easy victory.

The Japanese, however, knew the treachery of the black sand on the beaches of Iwo Jima. From camouflaged pillboxes on the slopes of Mount Suribachi, they watched and waited. As the U.S. troops jumped from the landing crafts their boots sank into the ash and cinder and machinery rolling ashore bogged down on the beach. More waves landed and equipment piled up on the sand. With the landing force snarled in a giant traffic jam the Japanese commander gave the order. The silent hills instantly rumbled to life as the Japanese emerged from hiding and opened fire. U.S. troops had fallen into a trap. On the open beach they had no cover except the bodies of fallen comrades and disabled vehicles.

Japanese ingenuity, however, was no match for the fierce determination of the Marines and the amazing accuracy of their fire power. The landing Marines concealed a secret weapon within their ranks—a select group of Navajo* Marines who uttered

---

* Long known as the Navajo, this was not the people's traditional name for themselves. In recent times, some Navajo have returned to using Dine (Dineh), meaning "the people." Because the nature of this book is historical, the term Navajo has been used.

A traffic jam occurred on the beach on Iwo Jima during landing. *(National Archives Photo #26-G-4474)*

sounds no Japanese could understand and no one except another Code Talker could decipher. Under heavy combat fire as they inched their way up the slopes of Iwo Jima these unique Marines transmitted messages night and day. During the first 48 hours, the Navajo Code Talkers coded and decoded 800 messages without error. After three days of bloody battle, when the American flag was raised on Suribachi, the news was transmitted throughout the Pacific in Navajo Code.

War was not new to the Navajo. Through the centuries, many brave warriors have given their lives in protecting the Navajo lands that lie between the four sacred mountains in what is now the southwestern United States. For generations the Navajo successfully defended themselves and their land from other tribes, the Spanish, and the Mexicans. After the signing of the Treaty of Guadalupe Hidalgo in 1848, Mexico ceded Upper California and New Mexico Territory (including Arizona) to the United States, and the Navajo sacred land became U.S. territory.

The Navajo, not consulted in the negotiation of the treaty, continued living their traditional lifestyle. They grew corn, raised sheep and wove the wool into beautifully designed blankets and rugs. Along with the other tribes in the area they had obtained horses, which were not native to North America, through trade and by capturing wild horses. (The first horses had been brought by the Spanish in the 1500s.) The Navajo increased their horse herds by raiding Spanish settlements and other tribes. As American settlers ventured into the newly gained territory, they, too, were visited by Navajo raiding parties. In effort to protect the

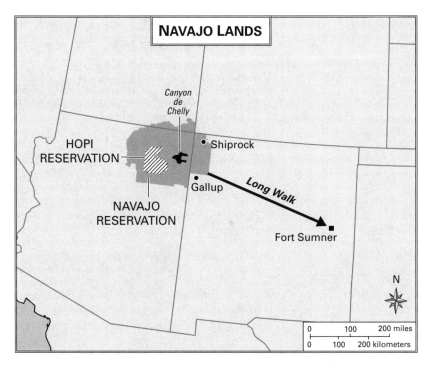

The Navajo made their last stand of the Navajo War in Canyon de Chelly. Forced to surrender, they made the Long Walk to a four-year exile at Ft. Sumner.

settlers, the U.S. government sent the cavalry to control the Indians.

As American settlement expanded, both the settlers and the Indians longed for peace—however, not in exactly the same way. The Indians wanted to return to the life they had known before the settlers came. The settlers wanted the Indians off "their" land and away from their families and livestock. U.S. officials began negotiating treaties with the Navajo. The treaties' aim was to control the Indians; little consideration was given to their traditional lifestyle. In addition, the negotiators mistakenly assumed that the Navajo had a single chief who spoke for the whole tribe.

The Navajo lifestyle and the vastness of the land made rule by one chief impossible. Extended families, or clans, lived in clusters of hogans (round houses made of wood covered with mud and clay) surrounded by grazing land for their sheep, horse, and goat herds. Each clan—a unit organized around common ancestry—was governed by a headman. Miles of sparse grazing land separated neighboring clans. A treaty with a headman was actually a treaty with only one of many clans. A neighboring clan would not consider itself bound by that agreement and might not even know that a treaty had been signed. When the neighboring clan then made a raid, U.S. officials assumed that the treaty had been broken. As the raids continued the cavalry tried to bring peace to the Southwest by rounding up the Indians. About the same time, rumors of gold in Navajo country brought strong demands for opening Navajo lands to prospectors. In the face of this threat, the Navajo rose to the defense of their beloved homeland. The resulting Navajo War began in 1860.

In January 1864, the Navajo made their last stand against Kit Carson and the U.S. Cavalry. The massive Canyon de Chelly, in what is now Arizona, surrounded by 1,000 foot walls with only one entrance, seemed like the ideal stronghold. However, Kit Carson and his men rode across Navajo lands and into the canyon, burning hogans and destroying crops, uprooting fruit trees, and killing livestock. This "scorched earth" policy created a barren land. By winter the canyon sanctuary became a prison for the surviving Navajo who took refuge there. Without food or shelter from the cold, the entrapped Navajo had no choice but to surrender.

This defeat brought the greatest tragedy in Navajo history. Already weakened by hunger and exposure to the cold, they were forced to leave their homeland and make what became known as the Long Walk to Bosque Redondo near Ft. Sumner, New Mexico. (Bosque Redondo was an almost prison camp–like area where Indians of many tribes were being held.) Hundreds died during the 300-mile journey. Upon arrival at Bosque Redondo, the Navajo found the area already occupied by the Mescalero Apache and others. In this strange and crowded land, with little food and shelter, many more died. Approximately 8,500 Navajo began the Long Walk; only 6,000 returned to their homeland four years later.

The Navajo suffered tremendously during this captivity and exile. Because the elders believed that the practice of raiding American settlements brought the tragedy on the Navajo, they vowed never to make war against the whites again.

In their book, *The Navajo*, scholars Clyde Kluckhohn and Dorothea Leighton described the aftermath of the Navajo's exile at Bosque Redondo:

> Probably no folk has ever had a greater shock. Proud, they saw their properties destroyed and knew what it was to be dependent upon the largess of strangers. Not understanding group activities and accustomed to move freely over great spaces, they knew the misery of confinement within a limited area. Taken far from the rugged and vivid landscape which they prized so highly, they lived in a flat and colorless region, eating alien foods and drinking bitter water which made them ill . . . Fort Sumner [Bosque Redondo] was a major calamity to The [Navajo] People; its full effects upon their imagination can hardly be conveyed to white readers . . . One can no more understand Navaho attitudes . . . without knowing of Fort Sumner than he can comprehend Southern attitudes without knowing of the Civil War.

The exile ended with the signing of the Treaty of 1868. This treaty established the Navajo Reservation on the Navajo homeland. As the Navajo began to recover from exile, they struggled until their sheep and goat herds increased. In time, trading posts

Young Navajo woman sits sadly during exile at Bosque Redondo. Wrapped in a Navajo blanket with her baby on her back, this woman's face reflects the pain and sorrow the Navajo endured during exile. *(Special Collections, Merriott Library, University of Utah, #3242)*

opened on the reservation providing the Navajo with the opportunity to buy goods and market their rugs and blankets. Demand for Navajo weavings increased, and traders encouraged them to create more designs. Their increasing herds provided wool for the rugs and blankets as well as meat for the tribe. With their vast homeland returned to them, many Navajo experienced prosperity, by their standards, until the 1930s.

In 1912, Arizona and New Mexico became states. The discovery of oil on Navajo lands brought more federal involvement in tribal affairs. By the end of the 1920s, the U.S. government became concerned that overgrazing on Navajo lands contributed to soil erosion. Concerns increased as observers linked the erosion on Navajo lands to silt-runoff problems at nearby Lake Mead in Nevada and at the newly built Hoover Dam on the Arizona/Nevada border. The large Navajo herds had, in fact, outgrown their grazing lands. Charlie Yellow, a Navajo medicine man, remembered this period as a time when the herds "grew to great numbers, and the ground became bare like the floor."

In order to deal with the overgrazing and erosion, President Franklin D. Roosevelt initiated the Navajo Stock Reduction Program. The Roosevelt administration planned to replace the traditional sheep herds with fewer hybrid animals that would produce more wool and meat per animal. Because there would be fewer animals on the grazing lands, the stress to the environment would be less. In order to make up for the income lost by the reduction in the number of Navajo sheep, the government hired Navajo to build dams, schools, and bridges. However, the plan did not work. There were not enough jobs to make up for the lost income. And, instead of gaining grazing lands by reducing the herds, the grasses died away and less desirable plants took their place. As the Navajo tried to protect their herds, each family settled in an area and claimed as much land as they could. They no longer moved constantly, spreading the grazing over large areas. Instead, a result of this change was the overgrazing of nearby grasslands. As government officials destroyed the sheep and goats, Navajo prosperity turned to poverty and people faced

LONG-DISTANCE COMMUNICATION

Since the earliest civilizations, people have found ways to communicate beyond normal hearing range. When shouts could not be heard, commanders of ancient armies signaled their troops with hand gestures, arm motions, fire, and columns of smoke. Century after century, though, distant communication skills showed little advancement. In 1776, the lighting of two lanterns in a Boston, Massachusetts church tower signaled to the waiting patriots that the British were coming by sea and triggered Paul Revere's famous ride. For the most part, the success of distant communication depended on the ingenuity of the sender.

Almost a century later during the Civil War, the Union Army saw the need for better military communication. Major Albert J. Myer was assigned to duty as the first signal officer and ordered to direct a full-scale communications operation. He developed a code using flags by day and torches at night for sending messages between military outposts. As a result of his success, the Signal Corps became an official branch of the U.S. Army in 1863. A flag code, semaphore, is still used today as an effective method of signaling between ships at sea.

Since then armed forces have used mirrors, flags, lights, flares, smoke, rockets, firearms, and bugle calls, couriers on foot and horseback, carrier pigeons, telegraph, telephones, radios, and satellites. While all these systems worked to get some messages through, the messages were easily intercepted. Most of the time, anyone watching or listening knew the contents of the message. The more sophisticated coding machines of World War II simply called for more sophisticated decoding machines—until the Navajo came on the scene.

hunger once more. The Navajo consider stock reduction another great tragedy in their history, second only to the Long Walk.

Since the Long Walk, more than 100 years ago, the Navajo have told the stories of these great tragedies to their children. Generation after generation, it has become a part of their tradition and a duty of the elders. They have not forgotten, nor will they forget, the sufferings brought upon their nation by the U.S. government.

Considering past treatment, it would be reasonable for the Navajo to refuse to send their young men to war to defend the United States. However, along with the memories, the Navajo have received wisdom from their elders. That wisdom tells them that their sacred land lies within the bounds of the United States. If ever enemy forces land on U.S. shores, Navajo lands are no longer safe from yet another invasion of foreigners. In their view, fighting to defend the United States is fighting to defend their homelands.

Although the U.S. mainland has been secure since the British were defeated in the Revolutionary War, American troops have fought to defend countries overseas. In 1918, the United States joined the Allied forces—Britain, France, and the Soviet Union—against German aggression in World War I.

The history of the American Indian code talker began in the Argonne Forest of northern France in October 1918. As the Allies struggled to defend France, they were overpowered and outnumbered by the powerful German army and defeat appeared to be far more likely than victory. American commanders of the 36th Division, 142nd Infantry, had been ordered to capture a German stronghold of Forest Ferme. A month earlier, in September, the French had tried an attack on the same German position and failed. The American commanders knew that a surprise attack offered their only hope for victory. However, surprising the Germans was almost impossible. The Germans were intercepting and decoding almost every message the Allies sent. The solution to this problem, however, lay hidden within the American forces. According to researcher Mike Wright, the discovery happened quite by accident one night as Captain Lawrence strolled among his men in Company E. He overheard Choctaw soldiers Solomon Louis and Mitchell Bobb talking in their native language. An idea surfaced and Lawrence immediately sought more information from Corporal Louis, a full Choctaw Indian from Oklahoma. "Say, how many of you Choctaw boys do we have in this battalion?"

Including himself, Louis immediately named eight men he knew who spoke fluent Choctaw. Captain Lawrence told Louis

WORLD WAR I LETTER

This letter from Colonel Bloor, written in 1919, details the use of the Choctaw code talkers in World War I:

Headquarters 142nd Infantry A.D. F.
January 23, 1919, A.P.O. No. 796

From: C.O. 142nd Infantry.
To: The commanding General 36th division (Attention Captain Spence)
Subject: Transmitting messages in Choctaw.

1. In compliance with Memorandum, Headquarters 36th Division, January 21, 1919, to C.O. 142nd Infantry, the following account is submitted:
    In the first action of the 142nd Infantry at St. Etienne [France], it was recognized that of all the various methods of liaison the telephone presented the greatest possibilities. The field of rocket signals is restricted to a small number of agreed signals. The runner system is slow and hazardous. T.P.S. [telephone system] is always an uncertain quantity. It may work beautifully and again, it may be entirely worthless. The available means, therefore, for the rapid and full transmission of information are the radio, buzzer, and telephone, and of these the telephone was by far the superior—provided it could be used without let or hindrance, provided straight to the point information could be given.
    It was well understood however that the German was a past master in the art of "Listening in." Moreover, from St. Etienne to the Aisne we had traveled through a country netted with German wire and cables. We established P.C.'s in dugouts, and houses, but recently occupied by him. There was every reason to believe every decipherable message or word going over our wires also went to the enemy. A rumor was out that our Division had given false co-ordinates of our supply dump, and that in thirty minutes the enemy shells were falling on the point. We felt sure the enemy knew too much. It was therefore

and Bobb to translate a message into Choctaw and relay it to company headquarters. Bobb used the field telephone to speak to Ben Carterby, another Choctaw, at headquarters. Carterby then accurately translated the Choctaw message back into English for the battalion commander. With the success of this experiment the Choctaws were immediately dispatched, at least one to each field company headquarters. Once in place, the men began handling communications by field telephone.

According to Choctaw records six others joined the communications force. In all, 14 men of the 142nd Infantry, 36th Division, Company E, served as code talkers in World War I: Solomon Bond Louis, Albert Billy, Mitchell Bobb, James (Jimpson M.) Edwards, Victor Brown, Ben Carterby, Joseph Oklahombi, Walter Veach, necessary to code every message of importance and coding and decoding took valuable time.

While comparatively inactive at Vaux-Champagne, it was remembered that the regiment possessed a company of Indians. They spoke twenty six different languages or dialects, only four or five of which were ever written. There was hardly one chance in a million that [the Germans] would be able to translate these dialects, and the plan to have these Indians transmit telephone messages was adopted. The regiment was fortunate in having two Indian officers who spoke several of the dialects. Indians from the Choctaw tribe were chosen and one placed in each P.C.

The first use of the Indians was made in ordering a delicate withdrawal of two companies of the 2nd Ba. from Chufilly to Chardeny on the night of October 26th. This movement was completed without mishap, although it left the Third Battalion, greatly depleted in previous fighting, without support. The Indians were used repeatedly on the 27th in preparation for the assault on Forest Farm. The enemy's complete surprise is evidence that he could not decipher the messages.

After the withdrawal of the regiment to Louppy-le-Petit, a number of Indians were detailed for training in transmitting messages over the telephone. The instruction was carried on by the Liaison Officer, Lieutenant Black. It had been found the Indian's vocabulary of military terms was insufficient. The Indian for "Big Gun" was used to indicate artillery. "Little gun shoot fast", was substituted for machine gun, and the battalions were indicated by one, two, and three grains of corn. It was found that the Indian tongues do not permit verbatim translation, but at the end of the short training period at Louppy-le-Petit the results were very gratifying, and it is believed, had the regiment gone back into the line, fine results would have been obtained. We were confident the possibilities of the telephone had been obtained without its hazards.

A. W. Bloor
Colonel 142nd Infantry
Commanding

Calvin Wilson, Robert Taylor, Pete Maytubby, Benjamin W. Hampton, Jeff Nelson, and Tobias Frazier.

On the night of October 26, 1918, Choctaw telephone messages were used to move two companies from Chufilly to Chadeney. The Allies made the move with no interference. The next day Choctaw code talkers sent messages to direct a major assault on the German stronghold at Forest Ferme. Colonel A. W. Bloor, commander of the 142nd Infantry, reported that "The enemy's complete surprise is evidence that he could not decipher the message." The Choctaw code talkers played a major role in the Allied victory at Forest Ferme.

As the Germans withdrew they left communication lines intact. Colonel Bloor, however, suspected that the Germans were still connected to the lines, listening. Still, he confidently took advantage of the captured lines, With the Choctaws transmitting messages, the Germans were not able to decipher one word.

The tactic proved so successful that the Choctaws were sent on a special training mission. While there, they were instructed to choose Choctaw words and phrases to substitute for the military terms that did not exist in their language. For example, in the field they had substituted the Choctaw words for "big gun" for *artillery* and "little gun shoot fast" for *machine gun*. The war was over before the trained Choctaw code talkers returned to the front lines. They were then instructed to keep their role in the war secret and held in reserve for use in future wars. (The Comanche, as well as Choctaw, used their language to send messages in Europe during World War I on a limited basis.)

Once German officials identified the language, they did not intend to be foiled again. In the postwar years, the 1920s and 1930s, German "tourists" and "scholars" visited American Indian reservations to study the culture. In fact, they were on assignment by their government to learn American Indian languages. By 1941, when America entered World War II, most American Indian tribes had been visited and their language thoroughly studied—however, not the Navajo.

NOTES

p. 5   "Probably no folk has . . . " Clyde Kluckhohn and Dorothea Leighton, *The Navajo* (Cambridge: Harvard University Press, 1962, revised 1974, reprint 1984), p. 41.

p. 7   "grew to great . . . " Quoted in Sam Bingham and Janet Bingham, eds., *Between Sacred Mountains* (Tucson: Sun Tracks and the University of Arizona Press, 1994), p. 173.

p. 9   "Say, how many . . . " Mike Wright, "A Brief History of the Oklahoma Indian Codetalkers," Norman, Oklahoma, 1986.

p. 10–11 "Headquarters 142nd Infantry . . . " Col. A. W. Bloor, commander 142nd Infantry, Report to Headquarters, "Transmitting Messages in Choctaw," January 23, 1919.

BIRTH OF
THE IDEA

On November 25, 1941, a 28-ship task force including six Japanese carriers sailed from Tankan Bay on a secret mission. Observing radio silence, they followed a northern course between the Aleutian and Midway islands. Unseen by U.S. air patrols, they sailed toward a point within bomber range of Oahu in the Hawaiian Islands.

On December 1 (Tokyo time), the Japanese sent the first of two vital messages. On hearing the code words "east, wind, rain" in a Radio Tokyo weather report, all Japanese diplomats and consular agents in the United States destroyed their cryptographic equipment, code books, and secret documents. The second coded message, "climb mount Nitaka," transmitted on December 2, ordered a surprise attack on a U.S. military complex. According to the plan, the warships refueled at sea and steamed toward their destination.

Captain Mitsuo Fuchida, a Japanese bomber pilot, later wrote, "We were 230 miles due north of Oahu shortly before dawn on December 7 when the carriers turned and headed into the northerly wind." With the carriers positioned for takeoff, Captain Fuchida gave the signal, and within 15 minutes the 43 fighters, 49 level bombers, 51 dive bombers, and 40 torpedo planes under his command were airborne. They circled the task force, then slid into formation and set their course due south—destination Pearl Harbor.

At 7:50 A.M., the first wave of Japanese planes swept over the military complex on Oahu. Achieving complete surprise, they destroyed most of the U.S. aircraft on the ground at Hickam Field, Wheeler Field, and Ford Island, then bombed and torpedoed the ships at anchor in Pearl Harbor.

During the two-hour attack, Japan delivered a massive blow to the U.S. Pacific Fleet. Of the eight battleships that were in port, the *Arizona, West Virginia,* and *California* sank. The *Oklahoma* capsized; the *Nevada* was heavily damaged; and the *Maryland, Pennsylvania,* and *Tennessee* received light damage. Of the smaller ships in port, several were damaged beyond repair and salvaged for parts. Some received light damage and many escaped completely. Fortunately, no carriers were in the port.

Billowing smoke blackens the Sunday morning sky as firefighters try to douse flames that engulf battleships after the surprise attack on Pearl Harbor. *(National Archives Photo# 80-G-19947)*

The Japanese task force carried out the surprise attack on Pearl Harbor that drew America into World War II by sailing north from the Kurile Islands toward the Aleutian Islands, on east past the Midway Islands, and then south toward Oahu in the Hawaiian Islands and Pearl Harbor.

At the nearby airfields, few aircraft escaped damage; most were destroyed on the tarmac. More than 1,000 Americans were injured, and 2,403 lost their lives on that Sunday morning. Six of the battleships were eventually repaired and returned to the fleet. The *Oklahoma* was raised but found to be damaged beyond repair. The *Arizona* rests where it sank and serves as a tomb for crew members who died on board.

With few losses (100 casualties, 29 planes, and five midget submarines) the Japanese returned home in victory. As news of the attack reached the U.S. mainland, however, Americans went into action. President Franklin D. Roosevelt asked Congress to declare war on Japan the next day, which they did. Germany and Italy declared war on the United States before the end of the week. With the country suddenly at war on all fronts, patriotism stirred in the hearts of Americans. Volunteers flocked to military recruitment offices to enlist. With no recruitment office on the reservation, dozens of Navajo men gathered outside their superintendent's office, armed with hunting rifles, ready to fight the enemy. They were sent home because the draft call had not yet gone out and enlistment procedures had not been established for the reservation.

In 1941, many Navajo were already serving in the military. Like other Americans, they enlisted for many reasons. Many had not been off the reservation and wanted a chance to see the world. Others wanted education and training. Many wanted employment. Wilson Keedah Sr. who became a Navajo Code Talker said, "I went to war because there were no jobs on the reservation." The strongest force that drew men across America to recruiting offices after the Japanese attack, however, was patriotism. David E. Patterson, another Navajo Code Talker, gave his reason for enlisting, "When I was inducted into the service, one of the commitments I made was that I was willing to die for my country—the U.S., the Navajo Nation, and my family." Code Talker Pahe D. Yazzie simply stated, "I volunteered to serve my country."

Still, when news of the bombing of Pearl Harbor reached the Navajo reservation some of the younger Navajo wondered what it meant to them. At that time, Keith Little attended boarding school on the reservation at Ganado, Arizona. On that fateful Sunday, Keith and his friends went hunting in preparation for a Navajo-style cookout. While a rabbit roasted over their campfire, one of the boys went to the dorm and came back with the news that Pearl Harbor had been bombed. The 15- and 16-year-old Navajos discussed where Pearl Harbor was and who had bombed it; then, why. They came to the conclusion that the Japanese wanted to kill all Americans, including them. They made a vow to each other that they would use their .22 rifles to "go after the Japanese instead of hunting rabbits."

ON THE NAVAJO RESOLUTION

When news of the attack on Pearl Harbor reached the Navajo reservation, the decision that Navajo men would defend America had already been made. On June 3, 1940, the Navajo Tribal Council at Window Rock unanimously had passed the following resolution:

> Whereas, the Navajo Tribal Council and the 50,000 people we represent, cannot fail to recognize the crisis now facing the world in the threat of foreign invasion and the destruction of the great liberties and benefits which we enjoy on the reservation, and
> Whereas, there exists no purer concentration of Americanism that among the First Americans, and
> Whereas, it has become common practice to attempt national destruction through the sowing of seeds of treachery among minority groups such as ours, and
> Whereas, we hereby serve notice that any un-American movement among our people will be resented and dealt with severely, and
> Now, Therefore, we resolve that the Navajo Indians stand ready as they did in 1918, to aid and defend our Government and its institutions against all subversive and armed conflict and pledge our loyalty to the system which recognizes minority rights and a way of life that has placed us among the great people of our race.

Tribal council chairman J. C. Morgan and vice-chairman Howard Gorman signed the resolution.

The events of December 7, 1941 thrust a militarily disadvantaged America into a battle for its own sovereignty. With the U.S. Pacific Fleet successfully crippled in the attack on Pearl Harbor, Japanese aggression expanded south with air attacks on Manila, Shanghai, Singapore, and Hong Kong. Thailand signed a treaty of alliance with Japan on December 9, and the following day Japanese troops went ashore on Luzon, the northern island of the Philippines. By the end of January 1942, the Japanese offensive was well ahead of schedule. With American forces near defeat, the Japanese goal of dominating the Pacific appeared to be within reach.

In the following months, morale fell on the home front but patriotism soared. Americans who could not go to war flocked to the factories and plants. Navajos also contributed to the labor force. American automobile manufacturers shut down production and retooled their plants. Soon a steady stream of tanks and jeeps rolled off the assembly lines. All key industries worked 24 hours a day, seven days a week to produce a steady stream of artillery, machine guns, rifles, and landing craft. Americans invested their savings in War Bonds to finance the war and arm the troops with a winning arsenal. Military might backed by patriotism and courage, however, was not enough.

In an effort to stop the aggression in the South Pacific, America battled the Japanese on hundreds of islands spread over thousands of miles of ocean. Battle situations changed moment by moment, making communication links vital. During island landings, communications specialists carried radios and telephone equipment with them. Combat conditions allowed no time for complicated coding and decoding.

As soon as a position had been secured, telephone lines were laid to provide contact between the outpost and the company command post. Codes were used because almost all radio and many telephone messages were intercepted. Within hours after either side created a new battlefield code, the other usually cracked it. An unbreakable code would be of tremendous value. Ironically, it would not be highly educated, highly trained people who would provide this strategic edge.

The successful use of the Choctaw in World War I encouraged the U.S. military to consider further use of Indian languages. The army conducted limited testing at the beginning of World War II. In fact, some Indian code talkers were used by the army in combat in Europe. Today, the National Cryptologic Museum at the National Security Agency in Maryland, houses an exhibit that recognizes Comanches, Choctaws, Kiowas, Winnebagos, Seminoles, Navajos, Hopis, and Cherokees as army code talkers during World War II.

Comanche participated in the D-Day landing on Normandy beach in France on June 6, 1944. Forrest Kassanaviod, a Comanche who used his native language during the invasion, reminisced almost 50 years later, recounting that his memories of the war were not all sad. "There was some joy in the fact that we served this country of ours," he said.

Indian languages might have been more widely used except that some high-ranking military men in Washington were reluctant to approve their use for combat communication. They were concerned that static and combat noise might hamper accuracy. Also, Indian vocabularies did not include military and technical terms. These Washington officials were convinced that an unbreakable combat code was impossible. They believed the best hope lay in creating new codes based on the English language.

The United States might have missed an important strategic advantage if it weren't for a World War I veteran who convinced some high-ranking Marines in San Diego that a certain Indian language could be used to create an unbreakable code.

In February 1942, Philip Johnston read in *The Masterkey* about army maneuvers in Louisiana where Indians from tribes in Wisconsin and Michigan were used as "code transmitters." These Indians received "instructions in English, put them on the air in a tongue intelligible only to their listening fellow-tribesmen, who in turn retranslate the message into English at the receiving end." Johnston began to tie this information to his childhood experience as the son of missionaries living on the Navajo reservation. With only Navajo children for playmates, young Philip soon learned the difficult language.

Johnston linked his knowledge of Navajo culture and language to *The Masterkey* account of the Louisiana maneuvers and came up with a unique idea. The next day he drove to Camp Elliott, seven miles north of San Diego. There he contacted Lieutenant Colonel James E. Jones, area signal officer, and presented his idea. "What would you think of a device that would assure you of complete secrecy when you send or receive messages on the battlefield?" he asked. After a polite silence, the colonel leaned forward and quietly assured Johnston that in the history of warfare no code or cipher had ever been completely secure. Johnston continued, ". . . suppose we develop a code from an Indian language . . . One that

NAVAJO LANGUAGE

Navajo is a tonal *language*. Its vowels rise and fall and words change meaning with pitch. The pronunciation of some words includes a small clutch of the breath, known as a glottal stop. This slight hesitation, difficult for the English-attuned ear to hear, changes the meaning of otherwise identical Navajo words. For example, *tsin*, which means "tree," changes to mean "bone" when the glottal stop is added after the *ts*.

Because of its complexity and difficult pronunciation, only a few traders and missionaries had made an attempt to learn Navajo before 1942. They only learned enough to conduct their business and did not attempt to use Navajo in daily conversation. Only about 28 non-Navajos, mostly missionaries who had thoroughly studied the language, understood Navajo extensively.

Although an attempt had been made to write the language, it remained essentially oral. Furthermore, the Navajo did not adopt foreign words as other languages often do, and so the language remained pure. For example, when the radio was introduced on the reservation, the Navajo did not call it a *radio*. Instead they created a new Navajo word, *nil-chi-hal-ne-ih*. They also created a new word for telephone, *besh-hal-ne-ih*. These words are not pronounced as they are written here. Each syllable requires sounds that would need to be indicated by accent marks and phonetic symbols. Even with knowledge of phonetic symbols, an unpracticed tongue would have a great deal of difficulty. Deciphering a code based on the Navajo language would be significantly more difficult.

would always be used orally, by radio or telephone, and never reduced to writing that would fall into the enemy's hands?"

The colonel responded that the idea had already been tried and proved to be impractical. Johnston explained that his idea was not to transmit messages in Indian language but to build a code based on Indian words. Seeing some interest on the colonel's face, Johnston explained his idea further. He suggested that Navajo personnel would be thoroughly drilled and trained to use the code based on their language. Realizing that the colonel was not convinced, Johnston spoke a sentence in Navajo and asked if the colonel honestly believed that anyone but a Navajo could understand the words he had spoken. With the colonel's full attention, Johnston took advantage of the situation. He slowly repeated one Navajo word, syllable by syllable, and invited Colonel Jones to repeat the word. Johnston watched and waited. He knew that the varying tones and complexity of the Navajo language make it very difficult for a non-Navajo to repeat even one word. Jones twisted his English-speaking tongue and contorted his mouth. Johnston and Jones broke into laughter at the resulting sound, which did not resemble the Navajo word.

Suddenly convinced of the possibilities of the complex language, Colonel Jones asked Johnston to arrange a meeting with some Navajo.

Upon his return to Los Angeles, Johnston began a search for Navajo to demonstrate his idea. After contacting the Indian Placement Bureau in Los Angeles for recommendations, Johnston interviewed the best prospects for the demonstration. On February 21, 1942, he wrote a letter to Colonel Jones informing him that he would bring four Navajo Indians to Camp Elliott to test their language as a code.

In preparation for the meeting Johnston wrote a formal proposal for Colonel Jones's superior officer, Major General Clayton B. Vogel, commanding general, Amphibious Corps, Pacific Fleet, detailing the advantages of using Navajos to transmit oral messages in a code based on the Navajo language. Johnston considered fluency in the extremely difficult language almost impossible for anyone who didn't grow up speaking Navajo. Therefore, his plan included the recruitment of Navajo whose first language was Navajo. Although the tribe had a low literacy rate, Johnston believed that 1,000 educated Navajos, fluent in English, could be found if the Marines decided to go ahead with his plan.

Johnston and the four Navajos arrived at Camp Elliott on Friday, February 27. They stayed overnight as guests of the

Marine Corps, and the tests were conducted the next day. In preparation for the tests, Colonel Jones had installed a field telephone in the headquarters building and made arrangements for Major General Vogel and his staff to attend the demonstration.

On Saturday morning, Colonel Jones handed the Navajos six messages similar to those typically used in military operations. He gave them an hour to practice translating the messages into Navajo. Since the Navajo language does not have words that translate to military terms such as *dive-bombing* or *antitank gun*, the Navajos used the time to choose the words they would substitute for these terms.

At the appointed time, Johnston and the Navajos reported to Colonel Jones. He then took them to headquarters. After an exchange of greetings with Major General Vogel, the testing began. Demonstration messages were written by a member of Vogel's staff and handed to one of the Navajos. He translated the message into Navajo and relayed it over the field telephone to a Navajo who had been sent to another room. The Navajo who received the transmission translated it back in English and prepared a written message. Fifteen minutes later, the General inspected the translated messages. The accuracy of the messages convinced Vogel that the Navajo language could, indeed, be used for code purposes and he promised to pursue the matter.

On March 6, Vogel sent the results of the Navajo demonstration and Johnston's proposal to Commandant Thomas Holcomb, U.S. Marine Corps, in Washington, D.C. In the accompanying letter, he wrote that:

> The demonstration was interesting and successful. Messages were transmitted and received almost verbatim. In conducting the demonstration messages were written by a member of the staff and handed to the Indian: he would transmit the message in his tribal dialect and the Indian on the other end would write them down in English . . . The Indians do not have many military terms in their dialect so it was necessary to give them a few minutes, before the demonstration, to improvise words for dive-bombing, antitank gun, etc.

Along with the report on the demonstration, Vogel requested authorization to recruit 200 Navajos. Commandant Holcomb, however, referred the matter to A. H. Turnage, the director of the Division of Plans and Policies, for further review.

While studying the proposed project, Turnage discovered several issues that disturbed him. His concerns included the possibility of mistakes during translations. Also, he foresaw possible problems in teaching the Indians to use technical equipment. Furthermore, he thought using Indian dialect under combat conditions would slow communications. In his report, however, Turnage raised no objection to enlisting Navajos for communications as long as they also served as general duty Marines.

On receiving the report from Turnage, Holcomb decided to seek advice from the Bureau of Indian Affairs (BIA) before making a final decision. Lieutenant Colonel Wethered Woodworth met with BIA officials Fred H. Daiker, Lucy W. Adam, Dr. L. W. White, and Mr. J. C. McCaskill on March 25 in the office of the BIA commissioner. The BIA officials agreed that:

> For ordinary involved military communications the
> Navajo Language would be an ideal medium of commu-
> nication and that messages so delivered would not be in-
> telligible to anyone other than the Navajos themselves.
> [They also believed that] transmitting messages by this
> method would be exceptionally fast as the individuals
> could translate as they received and it would do away
> with any coding or transcoding of any sort.

After receiving Woodworth's report, Commandant Holcomb granted permission for the Navajo project. Instead of the 200 recruits requested, however, General Vogel received authorization for a pilot project using 30 Navajos.

NOTES

p. 13   "We were 230 miles . . . " Capt. Mitsuo Fuchida, "I Led the
          attack on Pearl Harbor," *Reader's Digest Illustrated Story of*

World War II (Pleasantville, N.Y.: The Reader's Digest Association, Inc., 1969), p. 19.

p. 16   "I went to war . . . " Quoted in Kenji Kawano, *Warriors: Navajo Code Talkers* (Flagstaff, Ariz.: Northland Publishing Company, 1990), p. 56.

p. 16   "When I was inducted . . . " Quoted in Kawano, p. 75.

p. 16   "I volunteered to . . . " Quoted in Kawano, p. 98.

p. 16   "go after the Japanese . . . " Bruce Watson, "Navajo Code Talkers: A Few Good Men," *Smithsonian* 24, no. 5 (August 1993), pp. 34–42.

p. 19   "There was some joy . . . " "Comanche 'Code Talkers' Reminisce on War," *Daily Oklahoman*, August 18, 1992, p. n.a.

p. 19   "instructions in English . . . " "Indians as Code Transmitters," *The Masterkey* 15, no. 6 (November 1941), p. 240.

p. 19   "What would you think . . . " Philip Johnston, "Indian Jargon Won Our Battles," Unpublished Manuscript, Philip Johnston Collection, Museum of Northern Arizona, Flagstaff, Arizona, p. 3.

pp. 19–20 ". . . suppose we could develop . . . " Johnston, p. 3.

p. 22   "The demonstration was . . . " Maj. Gen. Clayton B. Vogel, letter to Commandant Thomas Holcomb, March 6, 1942, p. 1, National Archives 1535-140 AP-54-dew.

p. 23   "For ordinary involved military . . . " Lt. Col. Wethered Woodworth, U.S. Marine Corps, letter to the director of the Division of Recruiting, March 26, 1942, p. 2, National Archives 1535-140 AP-54-dew.

THE ORIGINAL 29

Recruiting 30 qualified Navajos for the pilot program proved to be a difficult task. In many ways, life on the Navajo reservation had changed little as decades passed and, in 1942, horse trails still linked the hogans with the trading posts. Navajo commonly rode horseback or walked as far as 30 miles to trade their rugs and blankets for supplies. Still abiding by age-old traditions, parents practiced ancient Navajo beliefs and passed them on to their children. In fact, they had little desire for change or modern conveniences. Although the Bureau of Indian Affairs (BIA) had set up schools to bring formal education to the reservation, many children did not attend. Their parents kept them home to shepherd the flocks and tend the corn fields. Those who did not attend school did not earn English.

Fluency in the English language was a basic requirement for enlistment in the military. However, the "special duty" enlistment the Marines conducted on the Navajo reservation in 1942 was unique. Additional special requirements included fluency in Navajo as well as English. Neither pidgin English nor trader Navajo met this requirement.

By April many of the qualified Navajo, motivated to action by the Japanese attack on Pearl Harbor, had already enlisted. After meeting with BIA officials on March 25, Lieutenant Colonel

Wethered Woodworth described the situation regarding recruitment on the reservation in his report to the Division of Recruiting:

> [Of] some 4,677 males registered for the draft, eighty-
> five (85) individuals up to date voluntarily enlisted in
> some branch of the service and approximately two-hun-
> dred twenty-five (225) have been inducted under the Se-
> lective Service Act.
>   The Selective Service board in covering the area of the
> reservation has to a large degree deferred the induction
> of many of the tribe on the grounds of insufficient educa-
> tion. This has created a bad feeling in the tribe as on the
> whole they are most anxious to serve and be treated as
> other Americans.

BIA officials understood that:

> "Face" means a great deal to the Indian and that better
> cooperation and effort might be obtained if the individu-
> als recruited felt themselves to be singled out in an un-
> usual manner for an unusual job.

They strongly recommended that Marines recruiters seek the
support of the Tribal Council by acknowledging that:

> The services required are particularly valuable to the
> military effort and that the men employed will be in the
> status of specialist of an unusual order . . .

Further BIA recommendations included training the Navajos
as a group of specialists in Class V. Marine Corps Reserve rather
than sending them to boot camp and the continuing involvement
of the BIA and the general superintendent of the tribe. They also
made the unnecessary suggestion that Navajo interpreters accompany the enlistees through training (all the enlistees spoke English).

In making his decision to authorize the pilot program, Commandant Holcomb ignored most of the advice from the BIA. As a
result, Vogel received orders to recruit the Navajos as general duty
Marines who would go through regular boot camp training as

well as participate in the Navajo Code pilot program. If the first 30 failed boot camp, as many thought they would, the pilot program would end.

In order to reach the most educated Navajo, recruiting programs began at the boarding schools at Fort Wingate and Shiprock, New Mexico and Fort Defiance, Arizona. Marine Sergeant Frank Shinn set up his recruiting office near Navajo Tribal Headquarters at Fort Defiance. During the first few days, however, he received little response. Disappointed and discouraged, Sergeant Shinn contacted Chee Dodge, chairman of the tribal council. Conversations with Chee Dodge revealed that the tribe had not received notice of BIA sanction for the recruitment. The chairman sent a shortwave radio message across the Navajo nation and young Navajo men began to arrive at the recruiting offices the next day.

Carl Gorman was one of the first Navajos to respond to the call for volunteers. He later recalled that a friend told him that he had heard on the radio that the Marines needed 30 Navajo volunteers for special duty: "We didn't know what 'special duty' was but agreed it probably meant wearing dress blues and sitting behind a desk all day." Attracted by the prospect, Gorman rode into Window Rock the next day to enlist. Since the age range for enlistment was 18 to 30, 35-year-old Gorman listed his age as 30 on the application.

Age also presented a problem for 16-year-old William Dean Wilson. His teacher at Shiprock Boarding School encouraged him to enlist, but his parents refused to sign the consent form. One day, during lunch break, Wilson happened to be near the recruiter's desk. He saw the recruit folders stacked on the unattended desk and noticed his file had been pushed aside. A note attached indicated that his parents had withheld consent. When no one was looking, he removed the note and slipped the folder back in the stack. With this easy sleight of hand, Wilson became a recruit.

Cosy Brown enlisted because of a sense of tradition instilled in him through the stories he had heard of his grandmother's childhood experience on the Long Walk. Motivated by her courage, he

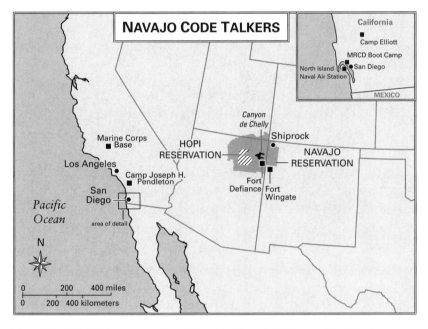

The original 29 left the reservation and traveled from Ft. Wingate, New Mexico, to San Diego, California, where they went through boot camp at Marine Corps Recruit Depot. Then they moved to Camp Elliott where they created the Navajo Code and trained as Code Talkers.

wanted to protect his people and the generations that would follow.

Whether motivated by a sense of duty or the desire for a better life, these men tried hard to meet Marine Corps requirements. The age limit was easy to overcome because the Navajo did not keep formal birth records. The weight requirement proved to be a little more difficult. Since the Navajo people are often small in stature, several of the young men fell short of the 122-pound weight minimum. Some stuffed themselves with bananas and others drank large amounts of water to add temporary pounds.

Within two weeks those who met the qualifications received notification to report to Fort Defiance for transport to Fort Wingate and formal induction into the Marine Corps.

Of the many who applied during the recruitment, only 29 made it into the program. Since 30 were authorized, many stories have surfaced raising speculation about the absence of the thirtieth recruit. George T. Hall, commanding officer, Marine Corps Recruit Depot, may have explained the mystery in his progress report to Commandant Holcomb, June 16, 1942:

> Twenty-nine Navajo Indians arrived at the Recruit Depot on 5 May, 1942 and were organized into a platoon . . . One Navajo Indian, Private Jesse Kennepah, (258451), who was in training when the group referred to arrived, has already been transferred to the Amphibious Corps and assiged special duty in connection with communications.

According to Navajo tradition, sending warriors into battle is a special event requiring a religious ceremony. As part of the farewell many families had Blessingway ceremonies performed for the young men who were going away to war.

The parents of Alex Williams, who became a Code Talker but not one of the original 29, called in an "old Navajo medicine man" to perform the Blessingway ceremony for him. Williams explained:

> [It is] mostly good luck prayers. And our medicine men . . . they have songs which they know only themselves. You have to pay so much . . . and then he'll take care of it with a lot of prayers . . . The prayers will be mostly the first night . . . the next day it will be kind of quiet, and they give you all a bath out of yucca leaves, and dry you then [with] the ground-up corn . . . corn pollen they use. You put clean clothes on, and you get the necklaces, belts, bracelets and so on, that the Navajo wear . . . The last night, all the parents and relatives and all, they come in and be there too if you want them to come, and then of course the medicine man will be doing his heart's worth, with prayers and then singing all night . . . They call it a goodwill thing.

After the ceremonies were over, the selected 29 reported to Fort Defiance, a few miles north of Window Rock, ready to enter a new

THE BLESSINGWAY CEREMONY

The Blessingway ceremony is the backbone of the Navajo religion. According to Navajo tradition, the Holy People held the first Blessingway ceremony when they created the first man and woman. This ceremony is used to bless the "one sung over." It ensures good luck, good health, and everything that is good—including beauty, harmony, success, perfection, well-being, order, and balance. It is sometimes referred to by English-speaking Navajo as being "for good hope."

The first night of the Blessingway ceremony several songs are sung. The ceremony continues the next day with a ritual bath in yucca suds and more songs and prayers. An all-night sing follows. The rite also includes the use of corn pollen, cornmeal and drypaintings created on buckskin using natural materials including cornmeal, pollen, and crushed flower petals. The ceremony ends with the *Twelve-Word* (stanza) *Song*, which includes the repetition of four Navajo words in each stanza that are believed to please the Holy People.

way of life in the military. They did not know when they would see their families again or if they would ever return to the land of the Navajo between the four sacred mountains.

On May 4, 1942, the recruits boarded a bus at Fort Defiance and headed for Fort Wingate near Gallup, New Mexico. After lunch in the dining hall at Fort Wingate, the 29 Navajo recuits were sworn into the U.S. Marine Corps. Following the induction ceremony, they boarded a special bus bound for the Marine Corps Recruit Depot (MCRD) in San Diego, California.

The original 29 made the journey without mishap and after arriving at MCRD they were given a day to relax and unpack before formally entering boot camp. Many years later, Eugene Crawford recalled in an interview that "After the free life of the reservation, this place looked like a prison with all the guards, gates and barbed wire fences." He wondered if the Marine Corps wanted to keep the recruits in or everyone else out.

Here, members of an all-Navajo platoon recruited in honor of the original 29 go through the infiltration course at the Infantry Training School. The smoke is from hand grenades.   *(Photo courtesy Defense Visual Information Center [DVIC], March AFB, #DM-SN-82-03214)*

Making themselves at home in the barracks reminded some of the recruits of settling in at boarding school. However, any resemblance to the life they had previously known ended there. The next day as they entered boot camp, most stepped into completely unfamiliar territory. Fortunately, Eugene Crawford had been in ROTC (Reserve Officers' Training Corps) in school and had some idea of what military life was like. He helped his fellow tribesmen adjust to the first few days of boot camp.

Under ordinary circumstances a Marine platoon consists of 60 troops. However, the selection of these Navajos for a special and secret mission created an unusual circumstance. As a result they were placed in an all-Navajo platoon, the first of its kind. Although singled out for unique duty, they were still expected to meet the high standards required of all Marines who graduate boot camp.

Marine boot camp serves to break the inductee's ties with home and civilian life while building a bond with the Marine Corps. The strict discipline and unquestioned obedience learned during this training period are designed to either make or break a Marine. Harsh as this training may be, on the battle field it saves lives. In boot camp, troops learn to stand at attention without complaint or question until ordered to do otherwise. They march and drill on command, eat and sleep on schedule, hike long distances as ordered, and participate in artillery drills and maneuvers. They also pull their share of kitchen and latrine duty (peeling potatoes and scrubbing toilets). A young man in boot camp makes no decisions on his own; he follows orders. Failure to carry out even the smallest order "as expected" by the commanding officer or drill instructor results in demerits. Acquired demerits must be "worked off" by additional duty or punishment that is usually quite uncomfortable and often humiliating.

The members of the Navajo platoon earned the normal number of demerits. However, Wilsie Bitsie, one of the smallest members of the platoon, earned the most. His offenses included being late for roll call, forgetting a piece of equipment during drill, failing to stand straight enough, and using the wrong term for his weapon

THE FIRST 29
382ND PLATOON,
UNITED STATES MARINE CORPS

Charlie Begay	David Curley	Chester Nez
Roy Begay	Lowell Damon	Jack Nez
Samuel Begay	George Dennison	Lloyd Oliver
John Benally	James Dixon	Frank Pete
Wilsie Bitsie	Carl Gorman	Balmer Slowtalker
Cosey Brown	Oscar Ilthma	Nelson Thompson
John Brown	Dale June	Harry Tsosie
John Chee	Alfred Leonard	John Willie
Benjamin Cleveland	Johnny Manuelito	William Yazzie (Dean Wilson)
Eugene Crawford	William McCabe	

(gun instead of rifle). He worked these demerits off by digging 6' by 6' foxholes, doing extra KP duty, and bathing Sergeant Duffy, a bulldog mascot who sometimes led the review parade at boot camp.

Adjustment from civilian life to the rigors of boot camp is hard for any young recruit and the Navajo were no exception. Cultural differences added to the difficulty. For example, Navajo consider eye contact rude and do not look into the eyes of others. The Marine drill instructor (DI) frequently looks individual troops in the eye and often demands that the recruit returns the stare, sometimes for long periods of time. In addition, Navajo seldom raise their voices to demand obedience. However, Marine DIs shout, loudly, often in a recruit's face. During this time the recruit must continue standing at attention. The DI sometimes asks humiliating questions, demanding louder and louder answers. Some Marine Corps Officers doubted the Navajos' ability to withstand the rigors of boot camp. The Navajos however, preformed so well that these doubts soon faded.

Although the Navajos may have experienced some difficulties due to cultural differences, their physical condition and experience of living in a rugged land proved to be an advantage during survival exercises in the desert. On one such exercise the Navajos and several other recruits were taken to the desert for a two-day march. Each recruit had one canteenful of water to last the two days. During the night, the Navajos used their knowledge of the desert and collected water from some nearby cactus plants. The next day, when the other recruits had drained their canteens, the Navajos still had water.

Through the rigors of boot camp, the Navajos had opportunities for fun that other recruits might not have had. During marching drill, one of them was asked to count cadence as they marched. The one syllable English numbers—one, two, three, and four—fit nicely with marching rhythm. However, Navajo numbers do not. Faced with the impossibility of keeping the platoon in step by counting cadence in their native tongue, the Navajos seized the opportunity to substitute derogatory remarks about the drill instructor for Navajo numbers. The DI was none the wiser, but the Navajos laughed so hard they couldn't keep their marching lines straight.

The original 29 recruits proved to be naturals with a pistol and rifle. As the Navajos prepared for graduation from boot camp, George T. Hall, commanding officer of the Recruit Depot, sent a progress report to Commandant Holcomb on June 16, 1942. In this report he gave the Navajo platoon a highly satisfactory rating:

> This group has done exeptionally well at this Depot. They are very tractable, attentive and loyal. At an early date they developed an exceptionally high Esprit de Corps. They have already fired pistol record practice: 76% qualified (general average for recruits has been about 70%).
>
> This group of 29 men is still intact, none has dropped back due to sickness, disciplinary action or lack of ability to keep up with the rest of the group. This is unusual. There is a usual attrition of from five to ten percent in ordinary platoons. Their progress has been highly satisfactory.

The all-Navajo 382nd Platoon graduated on June 27, 1942. They received praise from Colonel James L. Underhill, base commanding officer, as one of the outstanding platoons in the history of the Recruit Depot. He commended them for "obeying orders like seasoned and disciplined soldiers," their enthusiasm in learning new duties, and high scores on the rifle range.

After the graduation ceremony the new Marine Privates boarded a bus for Camp Elliott. The standard 10-day furlough given recruits upon graduation of boot camp was canceled and the Navajos went directly into their special training.

NOTES

p. 26   "[Of] some 4,677 males . . . " Woodworth to director of Recruiting, p. 3.

p. 26   "'Face' means a great . . . " Woodworth to director of Recruiting, p. 3.

p. 26   "The services required . . . " Woodworth to director of Recruiting, p. 3.

p. 27   "We didn't know . . . " Quoted in Ron McCoy, "Navajo Code Talkers of World War II," *American West*, 18, no. 6 (December 1981), p. 68.

p. 29   "Twenty-nine Navajo . . . " George T. Hall, commanding officer, Marine Corps Recruit Depot, progress report to Commandant Thomas Holcomb, June 16, 1942, National Archives 1535-75 AP-361-Cef.

p. 29   "[It is] mostly good luck . . . " Interview with Alex Williams, Marine Corps Navajo Code Talkers Collection, ms 504, University of Utah Marriott Library, Salt Lake City, Utah, p. 26.

p. 30   "After the free life . . . " Quoted in S. McClain, *Navajo Weapon* (Boulder, Colo.: Books Beyond Borders, Inc., 1994), p. 40.

p. 34   "This group has . . . " Hall to Holcomb.

SPECIAL
ASSIGNMENT

U pon arrival at Camp Elliott, the Navajo Marines were escorted to their barracks and told to report for duty Monday, June 29. Sunday would be a free day to spend as they pleased as long as they did not leave Camp Elliott. Taking advantage of the time for rest and relaxation, the Navajos played horseshoes and cards and wrote letters to their families back home. Although the Navajo Marines did not yet know what their special assignment would be, upon arrival at Camp Elliott they had entered a secret project with extremely high security. In order to protect the secrecy of this special assignment, the Marine Corps intercepted the letters the Navajos wrote and kept them from being delivered.

On Monday morning, after a seven o'clock roll call, the Navajos were escorted to the mess hall for breakfast and then led to the building where they would begin their special assignment. Bars covered the windows and locks adorned the heavy doors. Once inside, they were led to a large room that reminded Eugene Crawford of his classroom at boarding school where speaking Navajo was forbidden. He remembered being forced to wash his mouth out with brown soap as punishment for speaking his native language.

Crawford and the other Marines snapped to attention as the door opened and an officer entered the room. They relaxed slightly when they heard him say, "At ease. Please be seated."

Camp Elliott in 1942: The installation was located northeast of San Diego, east of Miramar Marine Air Station on Interstate 15. *(Courtesy Marine Corps Recruit Depot Command Museum, San Diego, California)*

In the next hour the officer briefly explained military codes; how they were made and used to code and decode vital messages. He told them that the Marine Corps had plans to develop a combat code based on the Navajo language for use in battle situations. Creating and using this code was their "special" assignment.

While U.S. forces struggled against Japanese aggression in the Pacific, every minute counted. The Japanese attack on Midway Island in early June proved to be a turning point in the Pacific. Japanese strategists had planned to finish off the U.S. Fleet in this attack. However, the United States had intercepted and decoded a Japanese message, giving them advance warning of the attack. Ready and waiting, U.S. forces delivered heavy blows to the Japanese fleet, sinking four Japanese carriers and equalizing naval power in the Pacific. However, more than three years of bloody war lay ahead and the United States still faced a very clever and determined enemy. The Japanese, as well as the Americans, excelled at intercepting radio transmissions and deciphering codes. Even as the United States tasted victory at Midway, further advantage was desperately needed; getting the Navajo Code into action remained a high priority.

In the classroom, the Navajos watched in disbelief as the officer turned and wrote the instructions for carrying out their assignment on the chalkboard. They were to construct an alphabet based on the Navajo language, choose Navajo words to substitute for frequently used military terms, keep the terms short for rapid transmission, and memorize all terms. Furthermore, all written materials used in the classroom would be locked in a safe at the end of each day. The men would also be kept under high security. They would honor the "buddy system" at all times. Whether on break for a stretch and fresh air or making a trip to the head (restroom), they would go in pairs. Leaving the building for any reason required permission, and they were not to discuss the project with anyone. The officer warned them that breaking the security of the project would mean spending the duration or the war in the brig (military jail).

At first the assignment seemed far fetched and impossible. Military code experts were not asked to create codes based on the knowledge in their minds. They used complex ciphering machines. How were 29 Navajos going to do this? They were new to military life and still making themselves familiar with military terms. Many of them had not graduated from high school, and most of them had not been off the reservation before joining the army. The assignment seemed overwhelming and unbelievable. In fact, some of the Navajos expected the officer to return and tell them their loyalty had been tested and now they would be given the real assignment. However, the officer did not return. Creating a code based on their native language *was* the assignment. Ironically, the language that they had been forbidden to speak at government-run boarding schools was now considered essential to the special service they had volunteered to perform for that same government.

After taking a few minutes for the reality of the situation to sink in, the Navajos began to discuss how they would go about the task. Facing the challenge of creating the code without a designated leader, the 29 Marine privates relied on teamwork. John Benally later said in an interview that "the boys that were in the original 29, Platoon 382 . . . they were the originators of the first interpretation of the code. I was part of that unit . . . and we all contributed to the code."

Each man contributed his special talents and knowledge to the effort. Wilsie Bitsie, whose father had worked on the phonetics of the Navajo language, suggested that they start with the alphabet. William McCabe remembered that Oscar Ilthma knew something

Only Navajos served as instructors at the Navajo School. (From left to right) Johnny Manuelito and John Benally, both of whom helped create the code and remained at the Navajo School as the first instructors; Rex Knotz, Howard Billiman, and Peter Tracy, who all became instructors later. *(Photo from Museum of Northern Arizona/Philip Johnston Collection, #MS136-IV-5)*

about words used to distinguish between letters of the alphabet that might sound alike during radio or telephone communication. Able, Baker, Charlie; Ilthma knew his father had used these terms and 23 others to clarify radio messages in World War I. In fact, they are still in use today. For example, in a telephone conversation "Bill" might be heard as "Phil." Misunderstanding can be avoided, however, by saying, "That's Bill with a *b* as in *baker*."

Bitsie, with his knowledge of phonics, also recognized the importance of establishing the pronunciation of each word to be used. Navajo is an intricate language made more complex by the fact that a slight variation in the inflection of the voice changes the meaning of a word. Like most other languages, pronunciation varies from one locality to another. Working together the original 29 agreed on uniform pronunciation of the code words just as soldiers coordinating an attack at a certain time might synchronize their watches.

As a team, they tackled the alphabet one letter at a time. Knowing the code would have to be memorized they chose simple words for common things: "ant" for A and "bear" for B. It seemed as simple as a toddler's alphabet book. However, as soon as the Navajo language came into play the picture changed. "Wol-la-che" meant A and "shush" meant B.[*]

As Wilsie Bitsie typed the list of the 26 words representing the English alphabet, he did not worry about adding the accents. The first instructors who would teach the code were among the original 29; they would know the chosen dialect and pass it on to future classes.

By the end of the first work day the first 26 words of the Navajo Code had been selected. The men repeated the coded alphabet until everyone knew it by heart. Completing this small portion of

---

[*] These Navajo words cannot be pronounced as they are written here. Many accent and phonetic marks are needed to represent the tone and pitch of each syllable and the many guttural sounds that are completely unfamiliar to the non-Navajo. The English alphabet alone cannot produce the true pronunciation or the true meaning. Even a Navajo would need to know which dialect was being used.

THE NAVAJO CODE ALPHABET

The first twenty-six code words for the English alphabet based on the Navajo language were:

Letter	English word	Navajo word
A	ant	wol-la-chee
B	bear	shush
C	cat	moasi
D	deer	be
E	elk	dzeh
F	fox	ma-e
G	goat	klizzie
H	horse	lin
I	ice	tkin
J	jackass	tkele-cho-gi
K	kid	klizzie-yazzi
L	lamb	dibeh-yazzie
M	mouse	na-as-tso-si
N	nut	nesh-chee
O	owl	ne-ahs-jah
P	pig	bi-so-dih
Q	quiver	ca-yeilth
R	rabbit	gah
S	sheep	dibah
T	turkey	than-zie
U	ute	no-da-ih
V	victor	a-keh-di-glini
W	weasel	gloe-ih
X	cross	al-an-as-dzoh
Y	yucca	tsah-as-zhi
Z	zinc	besh-do-gliz

the code encouraged them, and they began to feel they could accomplish the task. That night they fell asleep repeating the alphabet to themselves.

The Navajos knew the importance of the assignment from the beginning and sought to make the code as reliable as possible. After creating the alphabet they came up with 211 Navajo words to substitute for frequently used terms that did not exist in their language. Two reasons prevented them from making up new Navajo words for these terms: First, the code would be memorized for use on the battlefield and familiar words would make memorization much easier. Second, the code was needed as soon as possible, and creating new words would waste valuable time. In addition to choosing familiar terms, they further attempted to make memorization simple by using related or descriptive words. For example, Navajo words for officers referred to the insignia for the rank: "two stars" for major general and "one star" for brigadier general, a colonel was "silver eagle" and a major, "gold oak leaf." Other terms, however, could not be linked by description. Navajo words "salt," substituted for *division*, and "mud," for *platoon*, seem completely unrelated. However, these are Navajo clan names and have a definite connection for the men who would use the code.

When they began to find substitute words for aircraft, the job became easier. Birds seen on the reservation offered the perfect, easy to remember substitutes. Chicken hawk related well to dive bomber and owl to observation plane. The fast and mobile hummingbird reminded them of the fighter plane, and a large eagle carrying prey, a transport plane. They chose Navajo names of fish and water mammals to substitute for ships. The huge battleship resembled a whale and the beaver with its broad sweeping tail, a mine sweeper.

They also compiled a long list of terms frequently used in battlefield communication. They did not use substitutes when their language contained an equivalent for words such as area, available, column, and defense. Other words, however, required easy to remember substitutes or words that were actually Navajo synonyms for the English term such as:

English Term	Navajo Synonym
confidential	kept secret
conquered	won
establish	set-up
flare	light streak
hospital	place of medicine

Other Navajo substitutes were chosen for shape or resemblance such as:

English Word	Navajo Term
bombs	eggs
grenades	potatoes
route	rabbit trail
torpedo	fish shell
navy	sea soldiers
sailors	white caps
army	dog faces

At some point in building the code, the original 29 became overwhelmed in their attempt to find Navajo substitutes for military terms. When they felt they could go no further they asked for help from someone with more education. As a result, Major General Vogel assigned three additional Navajos to the program, Felix Yazzie, Wilson Price, and Ross Haskie. Price and Haskie had college educations. Ross Haskie, a teacher at Tuba City Indian School before he joined the Marines, graduated from Flagstaff State College.

After they completed the alphabet and list of 211 words, the memory work began. Memorizing the code, however, proved to be the easiest part of the Code Talkers' requirements. William McCabe, one of the original 29, explained the Code Talkers' remarkable memory this way: "Well, in Navajo everything is in memory. From the songs, prayers, everything, it's all in memory. So we didn't have no trouble. That's the way we was raised up." Carl Gorman explained it further, "We have no written language . . . we listen, we hear, we learn to remember everything."

Not only was the Navajo language well suited as the basis of a code but the Navajo possessed a memory and ability to concentrate during the chaos and crisis of battle needed to make them function as human coding and decoding machines. They were also dedicated to perfecting their skills and took pride in their contribution as Navajos.

In the classroom they tested and retested their ability to code and decode messages. They practiced sending messages that might be sent during combat, such as: "Landing wave on beach but loss high . . . " "Machine gun fire on right flank moving in, am forced to dig in . . . " In the first days of training they practiced messages of a few words and rapidly advanced to longer messages. They strove for accuracy in translating English to Navajo for sending a message and Navajo back into English as it was recieved. The coding and decoding went from the mind of one Navajo Code Talker to the mind of another.

During field trials the Code Talkers were amazed at how well the code worked. When they first realized they would be using their language to send secret messages, most of them thought they would just talk Navajo. Because much of the meaning can be lost in translating a message from one language to another this would not have been nearly as reliable. Exact meanings were needed for translations. According to William McCabe, "When we made that code . . . code within a code . . . the message comes out word for word on the other end, and including the semi-colons, commas, periods, question marks, everything. We get all those." By the time the original 29 finished their field trials the message received exactly matched the message that was sent.

NAVAJO CODE FOR MONTHS OF THE YEAR

Because the Navajo did not measure time as the Americans and Europeans did, their language had no terms for months of the year. They chose words that described the season or the events that took place at that time of year.

English Month	Navajo Word
January	crested snow
February	small eagle
March	squeaky voice
April	small plant
May	big plant
June	big planting
July	small harvest
August	big harvest
September	half
October	small wind
November	big wind
December	Christmas

The Navajos' mastery of coding and decoding messages surprised the Marine observers. Accustomed to machines that took much longer (often hours), they could not believe that the Navajos could instantly decode a message and suspected they were using some form of sign language. William McCabe told of one afternoon when a general came to observe. The sender and receiver were separated and given messages to send. Then a runner was sent to retrieve the message from the receiver. When the general compared the messages, he found a perfect match. Suspecting the Navajos had somehow given a visual signal he moved the sender out of the receiver's view. In addition, he ordered that a guard stand by to be sure the message could not be relayed any other way. Another message was sent and received. Again, upon comparison the retrieved message matched the original. Still skeptical, the general created his own message with a dash, comma, exclamation point, semi-colon, question mark, and a star. McCabe sent the general's message and as soon as the receiver finished writing the message a runner snatched it and brought it back to the general. Again it was a perfect match. The general expressed his surprise.

The code was fast and accurate but could it be broken? U.S. Intelligence tried and failed. During field trials the code was transmitted over radio and picked up by U.S. Intelligence. According to William McCabe they worked on it for three weeks, "They got the message but . . . there's no repetition, there's no sequences in there, there's no pattern" and they couldn't break it.

Once the original 29 began work on the code, they did not stop. Additional terms were added in the next class of Navajos and changes were made under battlefield conditions. In fact, improvement continued until the end of the war.

At Camp Elliott, while they worked on the code, they also received general Signal Corps training, which included Morse code, panel codes, signal flags, field telephones, and radio. They learned the mechanics of radio and telephone as well as the operation. They also received regular combat training.

They did so well in the pilot program that a few weeks before they finished training A. H. Noble, director of Plans and Policies, sent a memo to Commandant Holcomb stating that the Navajo Indians "have proven to be highly satisfactory and of proven value to communications." Based on the success of the original 29 recruits, Noble recommended that "that 200 Navajo Indians, having the qualifications normally required for enlistment in the Marine Corps, and linguistic qualifications in English and their tribal dialect which would make them suitable for use in the transmission of messages by voice, be enlisted." In addition, these Navajos would be "sent to the Marine Corps Base, San Diego, Calif., for the regular recruit training, and after that training is completed, they be ordered to the Fleet Marine Force Training Center, Camp Elliott, Calif., for three (3) weeks special course in the transmission of messages and basic familiarization with telephone and radio equipment; such training to be conducted on schedules prepared by the Commanding General."

When their code talking training ended in September 1942, members of the first class of Code Talkers were promoted from private to private first class (Pfc). Assigned to various units of the 1st Marine Amphibious Corps and 2nd Marine Division Communications Personnel, they shipped out to the Pacific theater as soon as possible.

NOTES

p. 39   "the boys that were . . ." Interview with John Benally, Marine Corps Navajo Code Talkers Collection, ms 504, Manuscripts Division, University of Utah Marriott Library, Salt Lake City, Utah, p. 121.

p. 43   "Well, in Navajo . . ." Quoted in Watson, p. 37.

p. 43   "We have no written . . ." Quoted in Henry Greenberg and Georgia Greenberg, *Power of a Navajo, Carl Gorman: The Man and His Life* (Santa Fe, N.M.: Clear Light Publishers, 1996), p. 60.

p. 43   "Landing wave on . . . " Philip Johnston Collection, ms 136-III-4c, Museum of Northern Arizona, Flagstaff, Arizona.

p. 44   "When we made that code . . . " Interview with William McCabe, Doris Duke Oral History Collection, ms 417, Manuscripts Division, University of Utah Marriott Library, Salt Lake City, Utah, pp. 8–9.

p. 45   "They got the message . . . " McCabe, interview, Doris Duke Oral History Collection, p. 11.

p. 46   "have proven to be . . . " A. H. Noble, director, Division of Plans and Policies, letter to Commandant Thomas Holcomb, U.S. Marine Corps, August 14, 1942, p. 1, National Archives AO-341-gmn.

THE NAVAJO SCHOOL

During the pilot program and the creation of the code, Philip Johnston remained in Los Angeles and continued in his job for the city. However, he had a strong interest in the progress of the pilot program that developed from his idea for a code based on the Navajo language. Late in the summer of 1942, Johnston drove to Camp Elliott for an update on the status of the program. By this time, the code had been created and successfully tested. In fact, the Marines were convinced that the Code Talkers would make a valuable contribution to the war effort. Recruitment of additional Navajos had been approved and the original 29 would soon be shipping out to the Pacific. In his conversation with Lieutenant Colonel Jones, Johnston indicated that he wanted to participate in the program. Jones immediately saw the value of Johnston's offer. Due to certain restrictions, however, Jones could not request Johnston's services or even pass his application on to headquarters. On Jones's recommendation, Johnston sent his application to the Marine Commandant in Washington, D.C.

Eleven days later Johnston received notification of the acceptance of his application. On October 2, 1942, Philip Johnston reported for duty with a rank of staff sergeant. He later noted in his files, "I was assigned to recruiting duties on the Navajo reservation for a month, and started training my first class in November." Carrying out his first assignment, Johnston arrived in

Phoenix on October 14, to begin a recruiting tour through Arizona and New Mexico. He then returned to Camp Elliott to oversee and plan the training of the second class of Code Talkers. Assigned to administrative duties at the Navajo School, Johnston did not attempt to teach Navajos to speak Navajo or contribute to building the code. He did, at times, act as liaison, or a link, to keep

Staff Sergeant Philip Johnston and Corporal Johnny Manuelito *(Photo from Museum of Northern Arizona/Philip Johnston Collection, #MS136-IV-1)*

communications going smoothly between the instructors and Marine Corps officials.

John Benally and Johnny Manuelito, two of the original 29, received exceptionally high marks during training and were asked to remain at Camp Elliott as instructors for the Navajo School. It was their duty to teach the code.

The eight-week course was divided into three parts of instruction. In the first stage the recruits memorized the alphabet. After they mastered the alphabet, they memorized the 211-word vocabulary list. They learned as many as 25 code words a day. The instructor drilled the students by calling out the Navajo words while they wrote the English equivalent on a test sheet. Drills continued until everyone in the class had mastered the vocabulary list as well as the alphabet. They were graded on spelling and penmanship as well as knowledge of the terms.

Second stage instruction used a Marine Corps training manual titled "Sample Operation Orders." Sample orders from the manual were translated into code and then read to the class by the Navajo instructors, Benally and Manuelito. The students translated from Navajo into English, printing the decoded message in English. These drills continued until the students attained satisfactory speed and accuracy in performance.

In the third stage, the last two weeks of training, the class went into field exercises. During this time they learned the operation and care of communications equipment, mainly radios and field telephones. Practice in sending and receiving messages continued and by the end of the eight-week period most had reached a high degree of efficiency.

While the second class of Code Talkers tested their skills under simulated combat conditions, Captain Stillwell, Camp Elliott cryptologist, monitored message transmissions and offered suggestions for improvement. He studied the code for repetition, sequences, and recognizable patterns in the messages. He suggested that the Navajos add two alternate terms for each of the six most commonly used letters of the alphabet: E, T, A, O, I, N. The code words for these letters became:

Elk	Turkey	Ant	Owl	Ice	Nut
Eye	Tea	Apple	Onion	Itch	Needle
Ear	Tooth	Axe	Oil	Intestines	Nose

In addition, he recommended one alternate for the second six most repeated letters: S, H, R, D, L, U. The code letters for these words were:

Sheep	Horse	Rabbit	Deer	Lamb	Ute
Snake	Hair	Ram	Dog	Leg	Uncle

Repetition of letters is one of the keys cryptologists use to break codes. Therefore, Stillwell suggested decreasing the use of the alphabet by adding more vocabulary words. Following this recommendation, the vocabulary expanded to 411 words. The additional terms included substitutes for the names of countries and additional military terms.

The Navajo recruits were instructed to use the alternates for each alphabet letter. For example, week might be translated into code as Weasel–Elk–Eye–Kid one time and Weasel–Ear–Eye–Kid the next time.

After the additions had been included in the code, Captain Stillwell monitored transmissions in the same manner as before. He was completely satisfied that the problem had been corrected.

By the end of the war many terms had been added to represent Pacific Islands and battles with the Japanese. The alphabet code expanded to three alternates for all except the eight least used letters; Q, S, U, V, W, X, Y, and Z.

Once the code was created and in operation, classes following the original 29 faced less pressure. Code Talker training still required long hard hours, but the second class found more time for relaxation and enjoyed other aspects of Marine life. They were Leathernecks (Marines) and Code Talkers. Proud of the uniform and the code created in their native tongue, the Code Talkers translated the Marine Hymn into Navajo.

Toward the end of their training, the second class of Navajo Code Talkers wanted to share their culture. They requested $20 from the Office of the Camp Athletic and Morale Officer to finance

THE MARINE HYMN

The Marine Hymn, a tradition that began early in the nineteenth century, boasts of the Marines' early victories. "From the Halls of Montezuma" refers to the capture and occupation of Mexico City and the Castle of Chapultepec, better known as the "Halls of Montezuma" after the Mexican War. "To the shores of Tripoli" refers to the Marines freeing American shipping from attacks by pirates on the Barbary Coast of North Africa. The author remains unknown and no one knows exactly when the hymn was written. Unofficial verses have been added after every war. In 1929, the commandant of the Marine Corps authorized the following verses of the Marine Hymn as the official version:

> From the Halls of Montezuma
> To the shores of Tripoli;
> We fight our country's battles
> On the land as on the sea:
> First to fight for right and freedom
> And to keep our honor clean:
> We are proud to claim the title
> Of United States Marines.
>
> Our flag's unfurled to every breeze
> From dawn to setting sun:
> We have fought in ev'ry clime and place
> Where we could take a gun;
> In the snow of far-off Northern lands
> And sunny tropic scenes;
> You will find us always on the job—
> The United States Marines.
>
> Here's health to you and to our Corps
> Which we are proud to serve
> In many a strife we've fought for life
> And never lost our nerve:
>
> If the Army and the Navy
> Ever look on Heaven's scenes;
> They will find the streets are guarded
> By United States Marines.

a ceremonial dance to be performed for everyone at Camp Elliott. Their request was granted.

The dance attracted the attention of the *Chevron*, a newspaper published by the Marines in the San Diego area. The resulting article hinted at the secrecy surrounding the mission of the Navajo

Henry Bahe Jr., Jimmie King, Ray Dale, and a friend prepare for a tribal dance they later presented to entertain their non-Navajo buddies at Camp Elliott. *(Photo from Museum of Northern Arizona/Philip Johnston Collection, #MS136-IV-3)*

Marines: "Not much can be said about the work they're doing in school and in battle zones. But it takes advantage of individual intelligence, military training and heredity, and is distinctly annoying to enemy forces." A few days later the *San Diego Union* carried a similar article: "Little reference may be made to the nature of their training at the Marine Corps training center at Camp Elliott, but their job requires individual intelligence and military training." The appearance of these articles caught the attention of Marine security officers. They immediately issued a memo to the Public Relations officers ordering tighter security on the Navajo project.

While this information about the Code Talkers appeared in the San Diego area, no news reached the reservation. Several months had passed since the original 29 boarded the bus for boot camp. During this time all letters home had been intercepted and withheld. With no word from their young men, worried families began to ask questions. In an attempt to obtain information for the concerned families, Dover P. Trent, assistant superintendent of Indian Affairs for Navajo Service, wrote a letter to Philip Johnston. In his reply, Johnston told Trent that:

> Navajos who have entered the Marine Corps receive seven weeks of basic training identical with that given to all recruits, after which they are assigned to our school for specialized studies. I regret to say, however, that I can supply no information relative to the nature of this activity, due to the fact that we are in receipt of orders from Washington placing it in the "confidential" category, and forbidding all publicity or discussion of the program with civilian agencies. You may already have a general idea of its character, since a limited amount of information was released by our recruiting personnel on the reservation some time ago. We hope, and have every reason to believe, that the Navajos will play a major role in Marine Corps operations. When the war is over, their story may rank with great sagas of the battlefield. But for the present, we are maintaining complete silence on the whole Navajo subject.

Although attempts were being made to maintain the security of the project, the general superintendent on the Navajo reservation, James M. Stewart, gleaned information from unrevealed sources and wrote an article about the Navajo communications project. He submitted his manuscript to Raymond Carlson, editor of the *Arizona Highways*. The June 1943 issue carried an article that not only revealed the existence of the Navajo code, but detailed its success, indicated the number of Code Talkers and named the instructors.

> A platoon of thirty Navajos . . . trained in signal work using the Navajo language as a code . . . performed their duties so successfully that the plan was expanded . . . by early December 67 new boys were enlisted.

The Marine Corps considered this article a serious breach of security that endangered the Code Talker Project and the Navajos already being used in combat. As a result, the Marines launched an investigation to determine who made the information available. The post intelligence officer, Robert M. Dergance, questioned the four men who had been involved in recruiting on and near the Navajo reservation who might have been in contact with James M. Stewart: Philip Johnston; Major Frank Shannon, officer in charge of Marine Corps recruiting in the area; and the two Navajo instructors, John Benally and Johnny Manuelito.

Johnston said that he had not furnished any of the information that appeared in Stewart's article. He further stated that he was fully aware of the importance of keeping the Navajo Code secure. He also reported that he had given information about the project to Major Shannon when he reported to him on his recruiting tour. However, Johnston testified that he had made Shannon aware of the importance of secrecy. Johnston wrote in his statement that

> While I was standing by awaiting further orders from
> Major Shannon (a period of five days) I showed him a
> file of correspondence relative to the Navajo communica-
> tion project, containing a letter from Colonel Jones with
> the sentence . . . 'for your information there is to be no
> publicity on this program' . . .

Shannon certified in a letter to the commandant that he had "at no time released any publicity, either magazine, newspaper or radio concerning reference [the Navajo project]," and went on to cast suspicion on Johnston, writing:

> It is noted that Sergeant Philip Johnston . . . was as-
> signed to the Recruiting District Headquarters, Phoenix,
> Arizona for a period of several weeks and assisted in the
> Navajo country in procuring of Navajos. It is further
> noted that Sergeant Johnston is a writer.

Benally and Manuelito both testified that they thought a Navajo who failed to meet enlistment requirements might have revealed the information.

The results of this inquiry were sent to Commandant Holcomb. From this information, Holcomb could not determine that any one person was at fault. As a result, he closed the matter by sending stern letters to everyone involved, warning them against any further breach of security.

When the second class of Code Talkers finished training and shipped out, Rex Kontz, Peter Tracy, Jimmie King, and Howard Billiman stayed behind as instructors. Jimmie King soon emerged as a leader among the Navajos at the school. He took the responsibility of making sure all Code Talkers met certain criteria. A Navajo assigned to the Navajo School after graduating boot camp did not automatically become a Code Talker; first the trainee had to meet King's standards. Language skills were important along with physical ability, intelligence, and character. King stressed the character issue because he considered code security vital. He said:

> We knew that a man had good character. You could trust that man. He wouldn't lie to you. He would lay his life down, just like we would, before we would tell what this (the code) was.

He recognized the possibility that Code Talkers might be captured and tortured in an effort to "make them talk." As a Code Talker instructor he "pounded" the necessity of keeping the code secret into everyone that went through his class. He said to them,

> You think that you love your country well enough that you'd lay your life down. Supposing that you were captured tonight, and they had a Samurai sword just cutting inch by inch and making you tell what that word meant, and then the officer would cut a little more . . . The minute you saw that blood begin to run, are you going to tell? Of course not, you wouldn't. You'd give your life before you'd tell this.

Jimmie King knew that thousands of lives would depend on the accuracy of the Code Talker's messages. Before he certified any student as a Code Talker, King was willing to bet his own life on that man's ability to code and decode messages in combat conditions. In combat, the coded messages often ordered bombing, strafing, or shelling so many yards from a certain point. An error in one digit could direct the fire at U.S. troops. Because of this possibility, King said, "I want it to be sure, and then be sure on top of that again, before I pass a man and say, 'Yes, this man is capable, he can be a code talker' . . . I knew that this man could be depended on 100 percent. There was no maybe and if about it. Trustworthy." Even with this high standard, the failure rate was extremely low, about 5 percent. Every Navajo who finally served as a Code Talker in combat displayed extraordinary perfection in coding and decoding messages under extremely distracting conditions.

NOTES

p. 48   "I was assigned to . . . " Philip Johnston, Philip Johnston Collection, ms 136-III-1a, Museum of Northern Arizona, Flagstaff, Arizona, p. 1a.

p. 53   "Not much can be said . . . " Philip Johnston Collection, "Navajos Readying to Make Going Tough for 'Japanazis,'" *Marine Corps Chevron*, January 23, 1943, p. n.a.

p. 53   "Little reference may be . . . " Philip Johnston Collection, "Navajos Ace Marksmen," *San Diego Union*, January 27, 1943, p. n.a.

p. 54   "Navajos who have . . . " Philip Johnston, staff sergeant, USMCR, letter to Dover P. Trent, assistant superintendent of Indian affairs, July 11, 1943, p. n.a.

p. 54   "A platoon of thirty . . . " James M. Stewart, "The Navajo Indian at War," *Arizona Highways* (June 1943), National Archives #2185-20, pp. 22–23.

p. 55   "While I was standing . . . " Philip Johnston, September 18, 1943, National Archives #2185-20, p. 2.

p. 55   "at no time . . . " F. L. Shannon, USMCR, Marine Corps liaison officer, State Selective Service headquarters, Phoenix, Arizona, letter to Commandant, U.S. Marines, August 24, 1943, National Archives #2185-20.

p. 56 "We knew that a man had . . . " Interview with Jimmie King, Doris Duke Oral History Collection, Manuscripts Division, University of Utah Marriott Library, Salt Lake City, Utah, p. 48.

p. 56 "You think that you love . . . " King, interview, Doris Duke Oral History Collection, p. 48.

p. 57 "I want it to be sure . . . " King, interview, Doris Duke Oral History Collection, p. 50.

THE CODE
TALKERS HIT
GUADALCANAL

6

By the time the original 29 were recruited, U.S. troops had retreated from the Philippines and retained only a toe hold on Corregidor and three smaller fortified Manila Bay islands. The flag of the Rising Sun, Japan's flag, flew over Hong Kong, Thailand, Malaya, the Netherlands East Indies, and most of Burma. Savoring these victories, Japan set its sights on gaining a position in the Solomon Islands.

Japanese forces landed on the island of Tulagi in May 1942. They quickly established a seaplane base there and immediately made plans for the construction of an airfield on nearby Guadalcanal. Allied forces, however, had broken the Japanese code and knew the Japanese plan before construction began. After gaining the information in July, they estimated that the airfield would be operational by mid-August.

Possessing the airfield on Guadalcanal was vital to both sides. The Allies needed the airfield to launch its island hopping campaign, a plan to drive the Japanese out of the South Pacific by securing and holding one small island at a time. And, with the advantage of the planned airfield, Japan could cut the vital supply line between U.S. forces and Australia, eliminating the threat to the expanding Japanese empire.

In preparation for the assault on the Solomon Islands, the Marines transferred Major General Clayton B. Vogel, the officer who initiated the Code Talker program, to New Zealand. Once there, Vogel helped coordinate the first amphibious assault in the South Pacific campaign—Guadalcanal.

With the Japanese airfield nearing completion, the 1st Marine Division was ordered into combat. They sailed with a huge landing fleet of 80 ships that reached the islands of Guadalcanal and Tulagi on August 7, 1942. The massive attack force encountered some fighting on Tulagi, but the Japanese offered little resistance on Guadalcanal. Caught off guard and unprepared for the attack, they took refuge in the jungle and waited for reinforcements.

As the Marines secured the area around the airfield, clusters of Allied ships lay offshore, their crews and captains exhausted from previous battles. Merchant vessels (commercial cargo ships called to duty to supply the troops) loaded with supplies and equipment crowded around the transport anchorage off Lunga Point waiting to be unloaded. Old Higgins boats (type of boat used to unload cargo) supplied the means for transferring most of the cargo from the merchant ships to shore. With no front ramp on these landing crafts, men offloaded much of the cargo over the side and then waded it to shore. Unloading the cargo in this manner required manpower and time, but with no apparent threat there seemed to be no need to hurry.

Japan, however, had no intention of relinquishing the strategic airstrip without a struggle. Rabaul, a major Japanese base, lay only 600 miles to the northwest. From there Vice Admiral Gunichi Mikawa, the newly installed commander of the Japanese Eighth Fleet, marshaled every warship under his command. The rapidly formed task force headed south, arriving at the entrance to Savo Sound in the wee hours of August 9. Under cover of darkness and while the U.S. crews slept, the Japanese slipped into the Sound and opened fire. Major Frank O. Hough, later wrote that,

> The loafing ships were suddenly blasted at point-blank range . . . In approximately thirteen minutes from the opening salvo, the heavy cruisers U.S.S. *Astoria, Quincy*

and *Vincennes* and H.M.A.S. *Canberra* were either sunk or sinking, and U.S.S. *Chicago* severely damaged.

With their protection wiped out during the night, the unarmed merchant ships set sail for safer waters that morning. They still held unloaded supplies and equipment in their cargo holds. The Marines on shore maintained their position as Japanese warships bombarded the island night after night. The Japanese also attacked the U.S. fleet and any supply ships that ventured too close. Savo Sound became known as Ironbottom Sound, as both U.S. and Japanese ships sank and littered the ocean floor.

While the naval battles raged, U.S. Marines lived in trenches around the airfield. The Japanese left on the island made life miserable for the Marines. Snipers targeted any movement above ground and commandolike units emerged from the jungle to

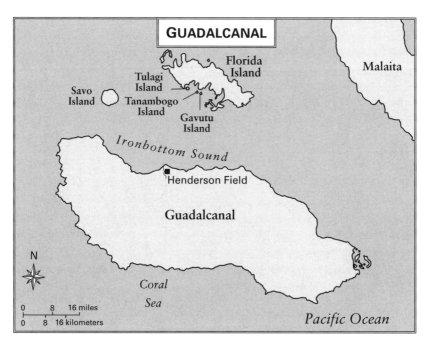

Many sea battles were fought off the shores of Guadalcanal, sinking numerous American and Japanese ships. In fact, so many ships littered the ocean floor that the waters between Florida Island and Guadalcanal became known as Ironbottom Sound.

attack without warning. Adhering to the Bushido philosophy (Japanese way of the warrior), preferring death rather than dishonor or surrender, they refused to give up. When ammunition ran out or defeat seemed eminent, the Japanese soldier drew his sword, screamed *banzai* and leaped into a foxhole to fight to the death. Richard P. Bailey, one of the first Marines to go ashore on Guadalcanal, remembered that he had not been warned about this Japanese tactic in boot camp in San Diego. He said, "They would rather die than be captured. Even when we took their rifles away from them they would try to kill us with a hidden knife."

Amid all this, the Marines carried out the backbreaking job of completing the airstrip. Remarkably, the first plane made a trial landing on August 12. Three days later, the first destroyer–transport ship reached Guadalcanal, bringing in the first supplies including bombs and aviation gas in preparation for an expected

GUADALCANAL

Guadalcanal, one of the largest in the Solomon Island chain, lies in the southwest Pacific Ocean between the equator and Australia. The tropical climate produces an annual rainfall of more than 100 inches and temperatures around 80 degrees throughout the year.

Roughly 90 miles long and 25 miles wide, the 2,060 square mile island has northern plains on which Melanesian peoples raise coconuts and cattle. Forests cover the southern mountains. The highest mountain, Popomanasiu, soars more than 8,000 feet above the plains.

In 1942, the Japanese occupied Guadalcanal, and the island became the site of the first important Allied offensive in the Pacific. After six months of fierce fighting the Japanese retreated and Guadalcanal became a major Allied base.

Out of a U.S. invasion force of 60,000, the United States counted 6,000 casualties including 1,600 dead. The Japanese force of 36,000 suffered 24,000 casualties. Guadalcanal was the longest battle in the Pacific. The bloodiest was yet to come.

squadron of planes. On August 17, two weeks after the Marines landed on Guadalcanal, the airfield became operational. It was named Henderson Field in honor of a pilot who died at the Battle of Midway.

The Marines holding the airfield were assault troops trained to storm the beach and gain territory to be held by reinforcements. They were not trained or equipped to defend a position for a long period of time. Still, they held their position on Guadalcanal seven weeks until reinforcements and supplies finally arrived.

Thirteen Navajo Code Talkers arrived with the reinforcements for the 1st Division. Privates First Class Charlie Begay, Samuel Begay, Wilsie Bitsie, Cosey Brown, John Chee, Eugene Crawford, David Curley, Ross Haskie, Alfred Leonard, William McCabe, Chester Nez, Lloyd Oliver, and Felix Yazzie were the first Navajo Code Talkers to see battle.

Upon arrival the Code Talkers had orders to report to the commanding officer, General Alexander A. Vandegrift, and no one else. Unfamiliar with the area and new to a combat zone, they set out to find the general. They confidently ventured away from the debarkation (landing) area unaware of the hazards on the island. They suddenly awakened to the reality of combat as they scrambled for cover when a Japanese Zero plane targeted them in a strafing run.

After their narrow escape, they found General Vandegrift. He referred them to his signal officer, Lieutenant Hunt. Hunt immediately decided to give the Navajo Code a trial. He assigned the Navajos to jeeps with radios and sent them in different directions. When the first words of the first message hit the airwaves, chaos erupted. Radio operators in the area thought that the Japanese had taken over their frequency. They immediately jammed the frequency in retaliation against the intruders. After this incident, Hunt delayed the test until radio operators in the area had been alerted.

This first exposure of the code to combat conditions indicated a need for an introductory phrase for each message. Before long it was decided that a Navajo message would be preceded by the words, "Arizona" or "New Mexico" to prevent panic among non–code talker communications personnel.

Later, Lieutenant Hunt scheduled a competition between the Code Talkers and a code machine. The outcome would determine which code system would be used, the new Code Talkers or the old reliable machine. Hunt boasted that the code machine could send a coded message and receive word that the message had been received and decoded in about four hours. When William McCabe said they could do the same thing "in about two minutes," Hunt didn't believe him. Hunt wrote a message for McCabe to send and started timing when McCabe picked up the field telephone. Two minutes and thirty seconds later McCabe had a "roger" indicating the message had been received and decoded.

No one understood how the Code Talkers could code and decode a message so quickly. However, it worked and the messages were accurate. That was enough for Hunt. From then on,

A Navajo Marine pauses on a South Pacific beach to use his walkie-talkie. *(National Archives Photo # 127-N-64081)*

any message sent from his command with a "secret" or "urgent" status was sent in Navajo Code. The code soon proved invaluable in jungle combat where units were easily cut off from the command post and the Japanese intercepted transmissions at will. They decoded most messages—except those sent in Navajo Code.

Code Talkers participated in every Allied offensive in the Pacific from Guadalcanal to Okinawa. In books about World War II written before the Navajo Code was declassified in 1969, Code Talkers were never mentioned. However, their individual names sometimes appeared in accounts of battles in the Pacific as they carried out normal Marine duties. They earned a reputation as good Marines who followed orders, did what was required of them, and used their natural skills to survive. G. R. Lockard, commanding officer, Signal Company, Special and Service Battalion, First Marine Amphibious Corps, wrote that:

> As general duty Marines, the Navajos are without peers. As individuals, and as a group, these people are scrupulously clean, neat, and orderly. They quickly learn to adapt themselves to the conditions of the service. They are quiet and uncomplaining . . . In short, Navajos make good Marines, and I should be very proud to command a unit composed entirely of these people.

The Navajos were also naturals at finding their way through the dark jungle, which made them good night scouts and guerrilla fighters. Accustomed to running in the desert, they were the fastest couriers. The Navajo were physically adept at survival in rough terrain and more able to meet the rigors of combat than were many of their fellow Marines.

Some aspects of their culture, however, made war very hard for them. To many Navajo an encounter with a dead body is extremely frightening. According to traditional Navajo beliefs the spirit of the departed lingers. These ghosts are believed to be a threat to anyone who comes near the body. In combat, troops are often surrounded by dead comrades as well as enemies. Under heavy fire, a Marine might spend hours or days in a foxhole with a deceased buddy. They often waded through floating bodies to body-littered beaches during a landing. For those with strong traditional beliefs, close encounters with the dead was one of the worst parts of the war until they overcame this fear. Code Talker Dan Akee said, "One of the most fearful things . . . to the Navajo was a dead body . . . I saw some dead Japanese . . . and I tried to glance at it [the body] . . . just couldn't help it, you know." He added that his fear of the dead was "one of the hardest things to get over. And I finally did . . . It don't bother me anymore." Another Code Talker, Paul Blatchford, said, "It didn't bother me, after—when we were pinned down, we were with a lot of dead Japanese and dead Americans. After that, after one night with them, why, I said, shoot, there's nothing to it."

Another Navajo belief was that speaking evil words during battle would bring bad luck. One Navajo Marine made a joke: "I'm getting fat and I eat too much. It would seem like the enemy would butcher me any time." The Marine's death in a Japanese air raid a few days later reinforced the Navajo belief.

Another Navajo belief forbids cutting hair before any important event, especially a battle. A lieutenant at the front insisted that all his men shave every morning. The Navajos in the unit asked Paul Blatchford to explain to the commanding officer that they couldn't cut their hair or they would die in battle. The lieutenant listened to the explanation and then volunteered to test the belief himself by shaving the next morning. Blatchford later reported the incident in an interview. He said, "So he did shave that morning and at 9 o'clock he got shot right square in the forehead." As a result, the commanding officer decided that shaving was optional. (Many Navajos have little or no facial hair. The beardless Navajos shaved only to follow orders.)

Adhering to tribal beliefs provided a feeling of security and eased fears of the traditional Navajo on the battlefield. Many of the Code Talkers brought pouches of corn pollen from home and carried it with them throughout their tour of duty. They used the sacred corn pollen in ceremonies they held among themselves in the South Pacific.

The Code Talkers sometimes used communications equipment like this battery powered Army TBX shown in the picture. In this three-man operation on Guadalcanal, the generator was tied to a tree and cranked to provide power for the radio. *(Photo courtesy Marine Corps Recruit Depot Command Museum, San Diego, California)*

Emotionally and spiritually strengthened by their beliefs, the Navajo fought bravely along side their comrades. Although none of them claimed to be heroes (seeking glory from war is not the Navajo way), accounts have surfaced of actions far beyond the call of duty.

In one act of heroism, Harold Foster saved his platoon sergeant. As the platoon marched along, they passed several apparently dead enemy soldiers. Suddenly, Foster saw that one was alive and raising his rifle to shoot the sergeant in the back. Foster said, "I had my knife all the time. I'm good at throwing knives, you know. I had learned it at home. So I just went like that and I got him through the neck." Foster saved the sergeant's life with quick thinking and the accuracy of his knife. It was done in the line of duty, however, and he did not receive any commendation for his action.

As the campaign for Guadalcanal continued, four of the original 29, Wilsie Bitsie, Eugene Crawford, Felix Yazzie, and Charlie Begay, assigned to the 1st Marines, joined the 2nd Raiders Battalion under Lieutenant Colonel Evans F. Carlson. This battalion became known as Carlson's Raiders. Carlson and his Raiders

THE RAIDERS

In January 1942, the Marine Corps developed the Raider battalions as a special mission force patterned after the British commandos and the Chinese guerrillas. Lightly armed and intensely trained, the Raiders arrived quietly in the night, sometimes swimming ashore from submarines. They slipped in behind enemy lines to operate as guerrilla units. Designed to take advantage of surprise, their quick and deadly raids inflicted heavy damage on the Japanese.

The first Raider unit, led by Colonel Merritt A. Edson, went ashore before the large amphibious landing on Guadalcanal. Edson and his men participated in the Battle of Bloody Ridge. The 2nd Raiders, led by Lieutenant Colonel Evans F. Carlson, landed on Butaritari Island, Makin Atoll, where their assault forced the Japanese to divert troops from Guadalcanal. They went to Guadalcanal a few weeks later where they stayed behind enemy lines for 30 days. The 3rd Raider Battalion commanded by Lieutenant Colonel Harry B. Liversedge, fought with the 2nd unit on Bougainville. These units suffered heavy damage during the two months they were ashore on Bougainville. The 4th Raider Battalion was commanded by Major James Roosevelt (President Franklin Roosevelt's son) for seven months and then turned over to Lieutenant Colonel Currin. The 4th Battalion slipped ashore on New Georgia and fought with other Raider units in a two-month campaign.

From Guadalcanal to Makin Atoll, to Bougainville and New Georgia, 5,000 Marine Raiders, with 18 Code Talkers hidden secretly in their ranks, became a legend in the South Pacific.

After the Raider Units were disbanded on February 1, 1944, the U.S.S. *Edson* was named after the commander of the first battalion, and 22 other U.S. Navy ships are named for men of the 1st Raider Battalion who were killed in action.

landed on a remote Guadalcanal beach on November 4, 1942, and began their famous Thirty Days Behind the Lines operation. During this time they carried out guerrilla raids against the Japanese.

For six long months U.S. forces fought to secure Guadalcanal against a fanatical enemy possessed by a win or die philosophy. The struggle finally ended February 7 when the Japanese left the island, "to fight other battles." Guadalcanal was a proving ground: the first United States ground offensive in the Pacific, the first taste of jungle warfare, the introduction of the Raider Battalions, and the first combat test of the Navajo Code. Lessons learned here resulted in improved equipment and training for the troops plus the first secure network of combat communication—the Navajo Net.

NOTES

pp. 60–61   "The loafing ships . . . " Maj. Frank O. Hough, USMC, "Action at Guadalcanal, 'Island of Death,'" *Illustrated Story of World War II*, (Pleasantville, N.Y.: Reader's Digest, 1969), p. 216.

p. 62   "They would rather . . . " Quoted in Sue Reilly, "Guadalcanal Diaries," *Los Angeles Times*, September 1, 1995, Metro, p. 1.

p. 65   "As general duty . . . " Commanding Officer G. R. Lockard, First Marine Amphibious Corps, letter to the commanding general, May 7, 1943, Philip Johnston Collection, ms 136-II-4.

p. 66   "One of the most fearful . . . " Interview with Dan Akee, Doris Duke Oral History Collection, ms. 417, Manuscripts Division, University of Utah Marriott Library, Salt Lake City, Utah, p. 6.

p. 66   "It didn't bother me . . . " Paul Blatchford, Marine Corps Navajo Code Talkers Collection, ms. 504, University of Utah Marriott Library, Salt Lake City, Utah, p. 115.

p. 66   "I'm getting fat . . . " Quoted in Lynn Escue, "Coded Contributions," *History Today* (July 1, 1991), p. n.a.

p. 66   "So he did shave . . . " Blatchford, Marine Corps Navajo Code Talkers Collection, ms. 504, p. 108.

p. 67   "I had my knife . . . " Interview with Harold Y. Foster, Doris
         Duke Oral History Collection, ms. 417, Manuscripts Division,
         University of Utah Marriott Library, Salt Lake City, Utah, p. 6.

THE NAVAJO
CODE IN
OPERATION

As confidence in the Code Talkers grew, Marine commanders in the Pacific began to use the Navajo Code to coordinate troop movement, direct land artillery, request bombardment from ships, and call for air cover from carriers. Concerns about the Japanese intercepting combat messages faded as evidence mounted that the Navajo Code completely stymied them.

Code Talkers arriving in the combat zone worked in teams of two. Sometimes they worked in shifts with one scheduled to work a certain number of hours and then rest while the other took over the duty. Sometimes they chose to work together round the clock. Periods of time passed when no messages were transmitted, but one Code Talker had to be available at all times. As members of the signal corps they were involved in setting up the communications center in the field. This included setting up the field headquarters radio, establishing telephone communications, and laying wire to the outposts. Roy Orville Hawthorne was assigned to the Headquarters company of the Seventh Regiment. Hawthorne said, "We'd work on the field wire teams and we'd go on combat patrols with the radio, of course . . . much of it was in the actual combat."

Code Talker cousins Privates First Class Preston and Frank Toledo send messages in Navajo Code over a field radio in the South Pacific. *(National Archives Photo #127-GR-137-57975)*

The Code Talkers were also sent behind enemy lines as scouts. They observed the enemy, noting his location, number of troops, and kind of fire power, and pinpointing sniper activity. They radioed their report and quickly moved on. Although the Japanese could not understand the code, they could intercept the message and identify the transmission site. Japanese artillery shells often blasted the vacated spot minutes after the Code Talkers moved on.

After the U.S. gained control of the strategic island, Guadalcanal became a staging area. Supplies were stockpiled there to accompany the troops on the island hopping campaign. Ships anchored in the harbor awaiting orders. Bombers and more fighter squadrons arrived at Henderson Field in anticipation of the next assault.

Since the code was secret, news of its successful use did not travel from one command to another. As each commander received Code Talkers in his unit, the Code Talkers had to prove the value of the code. The only way to gain the confidence of their commanding officers was to display the results of the code in action. Opportunities to prove their worth came unexpectedly and often during very perilous times.

One unit heroically captured a Japanese bunker, claimed the position, and moved in. No sooner had the Marines settled in than they were bombarded by U.S. artillery, "friendly fire." The men under fire radioed their new position and requested a halt to the bombardment. Since the Japanese were known to have held that position, the message was ignored and the shelling continued. The unit under fire called for a halt to the bombardment again. The situation was made more difficult because many Japanese who were educated in the United States spoke English with no accent. They often sent messages using very good English to fool U.S. troops. Fearing this trap, the message was again ignored and the shelling continued. After several more messages, the command post began to suspect that maybe they were shelling their own men. Still, they did not want to fall for another Japanese trick. Finally they replied with a question, "Do you have a Navajo?" The answer was "yes" and next words they heard were those of a Navajo Code Talker. The shelling stopped immediately. Although few knew of this incident, those who did had a better idea of what the Navajo Code could mean in a desperate situation.

Still, Marine officers were reluctant to turn secret messages over to the Navajos. By their very being they generated apprehension. New arrivals to the front, they were Indians, and they sent coded messages in a language their officers did not understand. Furthermore, the Code Talkers had orders of their own that complicated matters.

During training at Camp Elliott the Code Talkers were instructed to deliver the decoded message to the message center chief. That person was the only one below a lieutenant general (three stars) who was authorized to receive a Navajo net message that came into a command headquarters. The Code Talkers had orders not to talk about the highly classified code, or explain the coded messages, to anyone with less than three stars. Jimmie King said they were warned that, "There'd be new ones coming in, company commanders, battalion commanders, and other people

DISTRIBUTION OF CODETALKERS IN THE FIELD

By June of 1943 the Code Talkers had proved their worth in combat and the commanding general of the First Marine Amphibious Corps in the field sent the following recommendation to the commandant of the U.S. Marine Corps:

1. As the enclosures indicate, it is considered very desirable to continue enlisting Navajo Indians for duty in the Marine Corps as communications personnel.

2. The primary duties of these men should be that of "talkers" for transmitting messages in their own language over telephone circuits, as well as over radio circuits. Their secondary duties should be that of message center personnel (messengers). This designation will not limit their usefulness to the Marine Corps, however, as they have shown remarkable aptitude in the performance as general duty Marines.

3. The recommendation made by the 1st Marine Division as indicated in reference (a) is considered a minimum distribution. The following table is a suggested distribution and is also believed to be minimum requirements:

2 per Infantry and Artillery Battalion
4 per Infantry and Artillery Regiment
4 per Engineer Regiment
2 per Engineer Battalion
8 per Pioneer Battalion
4 per Amphibian Tractor Battalion
6 per special Weapons Battalion
6 per Tank Company
6 per Scout Company
8 per Signal Company

100 Total per Division

2 per Parachute Battalion
4 per Parachute Regiment
8 per Raider Battalion
6 per Raider Regiment
8 per Corps signal Battalion
8 per Corps Anti Tank Battalion
4 per Corps 155mm Artillery Battalion

A.F. Howard,
By direction.

. . . that will be questioning you." When lower ranking officers asked about the messages the Code Talkers were instructed to reply, "I'm not authorized to tell you what the message is about or what that man is saying over the air . . . May I have your name . . . ?" Awkward as it seemed, the low-ranking private first class Code Talker could send and decode messages that an officer was not authorized to hear or see.

Some Code Talkers were assigned to communications headquarters while others operated in the field. Independent and self-sufficient, these Code Talkers carried their communications equipment with them when they left the ship in a landing craft, scrambled up the beach, and trudged through the jungles. They were trained to set up the radio, set the frequency, send the message, and move on before they became targets. Marine radio men were usually equipped with a CR-300 field radio but sometimes the Code Talkers used the older army TBX radio. William Yazzie described this unit as an old clunker that had to be cranked by hand. When operated in the still of night, Yazzie and others were afraid the noisy cranking would give their position away. The TBX, however, was effective for long-range communications between the command post on land and ships at sea.

Under combat conditions the radios were subject to damage and as likely to take a bullet as their operators were. Code Talker Harold Foster told of being cut off in the middle of a transmission. "I was sending the message and that message broke right in half," he said. "So we started getting parts together to repair that radio . . . we were so pinned under that . . . [we were] praying at the same time."

Like every other Marine, the Code Talkers' lives were in danger during combat. However, when the enemy guns were silent, the Code Talkers faced danger from their own troops. Non-white, with straight black hair, dark eyes, small stature, and somewhat Asian-looking features the Navajo resembled the Japanese. Few people, Allies as well as Japanese, realized that American Indians served in the U.S. Armed Forces. Most people thought that U.S. military personnel were either black or white with no one in

To some, Japanese Admiral Gunchi Mikawa looks much like a Navajo. Because of similar facial traits the Navajo Code Talkers were sometimes mistaken for Japanese. *(National Archives Photo #80-JO-63697)*

between. As a result, Navajos were sometimes mistaken for Japanese. The situation was made more perilous because the Marines were always on guard against Japanese soldiers who sometimes sneaked into camp wearing uniforms stolen from dead U.S. troops. One of the first incidents of mistaken identity happened soon after the U.S. forces took Guadalcanal.

Marine and army troops had been on Guadalcanal a few weeks without many supplies. When supplies arrived for the army, Eugene Crawford saw a crate of orange juice being unloaded. He had not tasted orange juice in a long time so he decided to help himself. About the time he reached for a can of juice he felt a gun in his back and heard angry words that indicated he had been mistaken for Japanese. He identified himself as a U.S. Marine attached to the Raider unit located down the beach. The soldier responded with a nudge of the gun and ordered Crawford to raise his hands and move out. He marched Crawford at gunpoint to the Raider command post for identification. After this close call, Crawford was assigned a bodyguard.

In combat areas where the possibility of mistaken identity existed, bodyguards who would be recognized as being obviously American accompanied the Code Talkers everywhere. Crawford said in an interview, "If I went to the head, so did he. If I went swimming, so did he. He stuck to me like glue." Performing a vital and unique duty, the Code Talkers were in limited supply and could not easily be replaced. It made sense to give them added protection and the Code Talkers enjoyed the feeling of importance.

After Code Talker Bill Toledo was mistaken for a Japanese, a bodyguard was immediately assigned to keep him safe. From that point on, Richard Bonham stayed as close to Toledo as possible. When Bonham went on patrol, he assigned someone else to guard Toledo. After the war, Bonham reported that his unit had been informed "that the Code Talkers were a valuable weapon and their safety was first and foremost."

After the war, the Code Talkers were surprised to find out that the bodyguards had orders to protect the Navajo Code as well as the Code Talker. Not only was the Code Talker to be protected from mistaken identity; he was not to be captured by the Japanese. In the event a Code Talker was captured, the bodyguard had orders to shoot him. Fortunately, none of the Code Talkers were captured and none had to be sacrificed to protect the code.

JOE KIEYOOMIA

Joe Kieyoomia, a Navajo, joined the army before the attack on Pearl Harbor. Stationed in the Philippines, he became a Japanese prisoner of war (POW) about the time the Marines began recruiting the Original 29. Taken prisoner during the U.S. surrender at Bataan, Kieyoomia survived the Bataan Death March, an infamous forced march. Because of his Asian-looking features and his name, the Navajo soldier was thought to be of Japanese descent. The Japanese took him back to Japan where they hoped to help him return to his people. When this failed, they accused him of turning against his country. They beat him severely and tossed him in a cell. Badly injured with a broken wrist and several fractured ribs, Kieyoomia received little medical care in prison.

One day the Japanese had him listen to radio broadcasts. He couldn't believe what he was hearing. It sounded like Navajo but the spattering of unrelated words made no sense to him. He had no idea that the Navajo Code existed. When Kieyoomia said he didn't understand the message they accused him of lying. Angry Japanese guards stripped Joe Kieyoomia and made him stand naked on the parade ground. They hoped exposure to the sub-freezing temperature would make him more cooperative. In the 30 minutes he stood in the cold, his feet froze to the ground. When they forced him back inside for more questioning, flesh tore from his frozen feet. He left a bloody trail across the ground.

Kieyoomia endured months of torture. Even if he had been willing, he could not have given the Japanese any useful information. The code was designed so that even a person who spoke Navajo as his native language could not understand the coded messages. Only those who had received Code Talker training could decode the messages.

Held prisoner in a cement cell, Kieyoomia survived the atomic bombing of Nagasaki. Three days after the bombing, a Japanese officer released him. Kieyoomia returned to the United States and the Navajo Reservation.

The Japanese soon realized that the strange noises they heard on the airwaves represented vital information slipping past them. By 1944 their intelligence determined that it was Navajo. Unable to decipher the messages, they resorted to jamming the radio. They banged pots and pans, screamed, yelled and swore in an attempt to disrupt Navajo transmissions. Sometimes the Code Talkers drew the attention of Tokyo Rose.

Radio Tokyo used women with sexy American voices to broadcast propaganda programs designed to undermine U.S. morale. Tokyo Rose (actually several women) taunted American troops in the Pacific. She attempted to unnerve the troops by broadcasting details about U.S. troop movements. Before each landing she harassed the men with predictions of impending doom and descriptions of their death in the coming battle.

The Code Talkers played a vital role in the U.S. victory in the Pacific, and some paid with their lives. The first Code Talker casualty, Harry Tsosie, died on Cape Torokina. The Marines had dug in for the night, meaning that the men were in foxholes. The Japanese were close and very good at sneaking through the jungle, unseen and unheard. This made any movement above ground likely to draw fire. Striking a match to light a cigarette could prove to be fatal. The foxhole offered safety only to those who lay low and still. For some reason, Harry Tsosie left his foxhole and paid for that mistake with his life. The next morning they discovered that he had not been dropped by an enemy sniper; he had been killed by a navy medic. Harry Tsosie, the only Code Talker killed by friendly fire, was the only one of the original 29 who did not survive the war. He was one of eleven verified Code Talkers killed in action.

William McCabe witnessed the death of the second Code Talker to be killed in the war. It was so horrible that it didn't seem real to him. Ralph Morgan was standing in a foxhole with some other men when a shell landed nearby. The shell didn't explode but split apart on impact. Morgan died instantly when a large piece of shrapnel hit him on the chin and took his head off.

Code Talker Johnson Housewood was killed on a hill on Guam. He was shot when he raised his head.

Code Talker Tom Singer was killed in the landing on Peleliu. On the way in, Singer gave Jimmie King a message to give his family if he didn't make it. He somehow seemed to know Peleliu would be his last landing. Jimmie King witnessed Singer's death. They hit the beach together. King saw Singer fall and knew he was hit. Pinned down under heavy fire himself, King could see that Singer was wounded and bleeding. Any attempt to reach Singer, however, would have been certain death for King as well.

William McCabe had a close call on Peleliu. As the men readied to go ashore he was given the division flag and the privilege of planting it as soon as he got ashore. This was a dangerous assignment. The Japanese did not welcome the Marines on their soil and the raising of the flag always drew fire. As he left the ship, his friends said their last goodbye. Command had decided to use the Navajo Code 100 percent during the landings, and McCabe had orders to set up the communications post. He chose a site in a low area, a crater. While he worked to get the communications equipment in place, he laid the flag aside. Seeing this, his commanding officer volunteered to plant the flag. As he stepped to the rim of the crater and raised the flag he was caught in the crossfire of two machine gunners and cut in half. William McCabe would have met the same fate had he planted the flag.

George Kirk had a close call on Guam in 1943. He was on courier duty, assigned to a front line communications outpost. The outpost message center was actually a large foxhole occupied by a few dozen Marines. Kirk carried messages on foot from the front to the 3rd Marines' general headquarters. One day as he returned to the outpost after delivering a message, Japanese mortar fire came in and the message center took a direct hit. The impact threw mutilated bodies from the foxhole. Had Kirk been in the message center he probably would have been killed. He escaped serious injury and only suffered a concussion from a piece of shrapnel that pierced his helmet. Like many others, Kirk would never forget the horror he witnessed. He later related this experience to a reporter and added, "I saw one of the other Code Talkers there. Usually he liked to joke around . . . but on this day, I saw him cry."

Jimmie King remembered Peleliu as the place where his men suffered the most, where they went "the longest hours, without being relieved, without water, without even food and medical attention, and there were so many of them that got hurt." According to King, the Navajos were quiet when they were wounded. "They wouldn't yell. They wouldn't moan. They suffered silently."

NOTES

p. 71   "We'd work on the field . . . " Interview with Rev. R. O. Hawthorne, Doris Duke Oral History Collection, ms. 417, Manuscripts Division, University of Utah Marriott Library, Salt Lake City, Utah, p. 8.

pp. 74–75 "There'd be new ones . . . " King, interview, Marine Corps Navajo Code Talkers Collection, ms. 504, p. 59.

p. 74   "1. As the enclosures indicate . . . " Commanding general, First Marine Amphibious Corps, in the field, letter to the commandant, U.S. Marine Corps, June 22, 1943, National Archives Document 1535-140, AO-341-nls.

p. 75   "I'm not authorized . . . " King, interview, Marine Corps Navajo Code Talker Collection, ms. 504, p. 59.

p. 75   "I was sending the message . . . " Foster, interview, Doris Duke Oral History Collection, p. 5.

p. 77   "If I went to the . . . " Quoted in McClain, p. 89.

p. 77   "that the Code Talkers were . . . " Quoted in McClain, p. 104.

p. 81   "I saw one of the other . . . " Quoted in Paul Young, "Native Tongue," *Prescott Free Press*, July 1995, p. 3.

p. 81   "the longest hours . . . hurt." and "They wouldn't yell . . . " King, interview, Marine Corps Navajo Code Talkers Collection, ms. 504, p. 67.

8

THE CODE TALKERS' SHINING HOUR

After Peleliu, the U.S. forces moved toward Iwo Jima and the first assault on prewar Japanese territory. The island lay in the flight path of B-29s returning to the Marianas after bombing raids on Japan. These giant bombers, capable of reaching an altitude of 38,000 feet and speeds up to 350 miles per hour, could carry a bomb load of four tons. The four engine, long-range bombers could fly a 3,000 mile round-trip mission to Japan in 16 hours. On the way back to the Marianas, the bombers came within range of Japanese fighters based on Iwo Jima. The Japanese Zeros (fighter planes), aided by radar installations on the island, swooped down on the B-29s. With no emergency landing strip in sight, badly crippled bombers crashed into the sea before reaching base in the Marianas.

U.S. control of Iwo Jima would eliminate this threat from Japanese Zeros, and airfields on the island would provide emergency landing strips for the B-29s. In addition, medium range bombers could be added to the striking force and short-range fighters could be used as escorts during bombing missions. Air

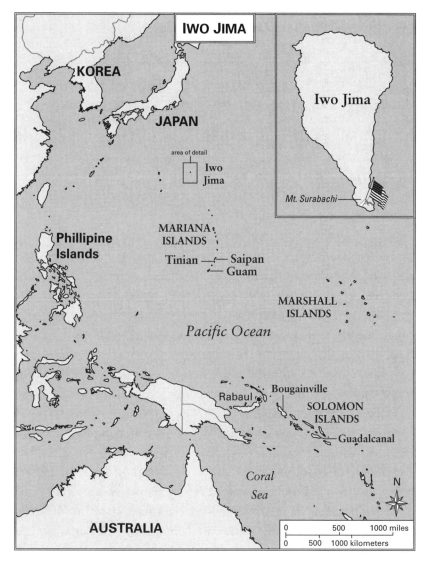

Iwo Jima is shaped like a giant pork chop. U.S. Marines captured Mount Suribachi at the southern most tip and then continued the bloodiest battle in the Pacific until the rest of the strategically located island fell.

and sea blockades of Japan could also be maintained from Iwo Jima. From this small, volcanic island—no more than a dot on the map—the destruction of Japan's air and naval capabilities was possible.

"Iwo Jima" means sulfur island. Barren and hot, about eight square miles of volcanic sand and rock, the island reeks of sulphur (an odor similar to rotten eggs). About 760 miles from Tokyo and vital to Japan's defense, Iwo Jima was a valuable asset the Japanese did not intend to lose. The Japanese leadership knew that once Iwo Jima fell into U.S. hands, Okinawa would be next, followed by the U.S. invasion of mainland Japan. Lieutenant General Tadamichi Kuribayashi, commander of Japanese ground forces on Iwo Jima, had orders to defend the island at all costs. He instructed his men to fight to the death taking as many American lives as possible. If the island were lost, Kuribayashi pledged that America would pay a high price.

As the U.S. force advanced toward Iwo Jima, Kuribayashi fortified the island with a network of tunnels joining underground concrete blockhouses and pillboxes. By the time U.S. troops landed on Iwo Jima, Kuribayashi had fortified the island with 800 positions for artillery, mortars, and automatic weapons. The Japanese also buried antitank mines in the island's sandy slopes. All this made Iwo Jima one of the strongest Japanese defenses encountered by the Marines.

Prior to the landing, U.S. forces pounded Iwo Jima with the longest, most intensive shelling of any offensive in the war. Commanders directed much of the operation using the Navajo Code. According to plan, the initial air raids launched from 10 carriers began in June 1944. Medium and heavy bombers later joined in a 10-week barrage. Three days before the invasion, six giant battleships, five heavy cruisers, and numerous destroyers began pelting the island with huge shells, five to 16-inches in diameter. By landing day, February 19, 1945, more than 6,900 tons of bombs and 22,000 rounds of naval shells had pounded the island. In readiness for the invasion, 450 ships massed offshore with 70,000 U.S. Marines ready to attack. As the hour of deployment neared, troop-carrying vessels moved into position about 4,000 yards from shore. This distance kept them beyond the range of Japanese guns on the island.

The first wave of Marines from the 4th and 5th divisions hit the beaches at approximately 9:00 A.M. The naval bombardment of the island continued, providing cover for the beach assault. Japanese guns remained silent and the U.S. troops began to think Iwo Jima would be an easy win.

> Up to the point of actually touching land, this operation went off like a parade. Then trouble started. The LVT(A)s found their way blocked by the first terrace, which rose to as high as fifteen feet. The volcanic ash and cinders afforded poor traction, and as the men of the first wave left their vehicles on the run, they were slowed down to a walk. A few amphtracs reached the first terrace through breaches blasted by naval gunfire; some backed into the water and fired their turrets at inland targets; but many bogged down on the beach . . .

After landing on an Iwo Jima beach, advancing U.S. Marines crawl up the slope, struggling for footholds in the coarse, ashy, black sand. *(National Archives Photo #127-N-110249)*

> As the Marines piled ashore they inched forward and
> took what shelter they could on the terraces, holding
> some momentum even though slowed to a crawl.

The landing suddenly turned into a massive traffic jam on the beach.

As soon as the protective U.S. naval bombardment stopped, the Japanese emerged from their fortified underground positions and opened fire. It was 9:15. Many of the men on the beach were mowed down on the spot. As those who survived tried to dig in, the sides of the holes they dug in the coarse black sand fell in. Trapped on the open beach, the Marines found no refuge except behind the bodies of fallen comrades and the vehicles and artillery that had been immobilized in the sand.

The Japanese had laid a trap for the Marines. However, they sprang the trap too late. A mountain of supplies and 30,000 Marines reached shore that day and more were on the way. The Marines held the beachhead as U.S. ships offshore resumed pounding the island with rolling barrages ahead of the troops.

The first Code Talkers came ashore in the second wave. Some of the landing craft were hit before they reached the shore. Merril L. Sandoval's landing craft took a hit and overturned. Sandoval survived but lost his equipment. He later gave an account of the early hours of the battle from his position, between the battleship *Tennessee* and shore. "The *Tennessee* was firing over our heads and the Navy and Marine planes were bombing and strafing Mt. Suribachi." He saw some of the planes fail to pull out of their dives and crash into the mountain.

Thomas H. Begay remembered his first hours on Iwo Jima, "The Iwo Jima sand was ashy and hard to walk on, but I had to carry my radio and other equipment across it." The two man teams carried their radios with them and the Navajo net quickly became operational. With observers ashore and the Navajo net relaying vital information, the ships could pinpoint their targets.

While the Marines were landing and consolidating their shore positions during the first 48 hours on Iwo Jima, six Navajo nets operated around the clock. Major Howard Connor, 5th Division

Signal Officer, later praised the Navajos for their accuracy during this critical time: "In that period alone they sent and received over 800 messages without an error."

Peter Sandoval, a member of a Navajo net, received messages in the radio room of a battleship during the landing. Messages were arriving so rapidly that he wrote a message, ripped it from the note pad, handed over his shoulder to a runner, and began writing the next message. After several messages came in, Sandoval ripped one from the note pad and told the runner to take it to the "Old Man," referring to the admiral. He paid no attention when the runner commented that it had been a long time since he had delivered a message. Sandoval was later told that the admiral had stepped in to watch the Code Talker in action. Sandoval had given the message directly to the admiral.

The admiral approved of the way Sandoval and the other Code Talkers handled themselves. Nothing seemed to deter them or shake their concentration when sending or receiving messages. When bullets zinged past them and mortar shells exploded nearby, the Code Talkers could be counted on to get the message through. It is not surprising that the presence of an admiral failed to draw Sandoval's attention from his job.

The Code Talkers on the island operated in the midst of fierce fighting. Advances were measured in yards as the Marines destroyed Japanese entrenchments one by one. Shells and bombs pulverized some. Tanks smashed the ones they could reach. Most, however, were destroyed by ground troops darting among the gullies, ledges, and crevices. Taking cover when they could find it, they maneuvered close enough to toss a grenade in a pillbox or plant demolition explosives outside a blockhouse. Flamethrowers seared the Japanese hiding in caves and tunnels. Explosives sealed the cave entrances to prevent Japanese reinforcements from attacking the Marines from the rear as they moved on.

> Iwo Jima is a story of yard-by-yard advance against a tough, resourceful enemy who allowed no let up, and who used his terrain as to extract the maximum price in

Marines of Easy Company, 5th Division, 28th Marines raise the small flag they carried to the summit of Mount Suribachi on Iwo Jima. The famous photo that won Joseph Rosenthal a Pulitzer Prize was taken of a larger flag that replaced this first flag. *(National Archives Photo #127-GW-319-116325)*

blood. The Marines advancing in the open with little natural shelter, had to fight their way against an enemy burrowed underground and protected from everything but a direct hit. It was a costly and exhausting grind, call-

ing for higher qualities of courage, initiative and persist-
ence than a campaign full of charges, countercharges
and spectacular incidents that raise men's morale.

The day after landing on Iwo Jima, the Marines secured the
southern end of the island and control of Motoyama Airfield. The
bloody battle continued with the Marines slowly advancing until
they had surrounded the base of Mount Suribachi. On February
23, First Lieutenant Harold G. Schrier assembled the 3rd Platoon,
Easy Company, 5th Division of the 28th Marines, at the base of
Mount Suribachi. The platoon climbed the steep slope, crawling
in some places, and reached the summit without meeting Japanese
resistance. At the top, some of the men took positions around the
crater to guard against any Japanese who might suddenly open
fire from a hidden position. Other members of the patrol searched
for something they could use to hoist the flag. At 10:20 A.M. the
U.S. flag tied to a steel pipe rose into view on top of Mount
Suribachi. A Marine photographer snapped a picture, then a
grenade rolled out of a cave and a few rifle shots were fired. The
flag raisers rolled to safety in the crater.

Code Talkers relayed the message throughout the Pacific that
the flag had been raised and Mount Suribachi had been secured.
It was a long message including: "Dibeh, Shi-Da, Dah-Nes-Tsa,
Tkin, Shush, Wol-La Chee, Moasi, Lin, Yeh-Hes" (*Sheep-Uncle-
Ram-Ice-Bear-Ant-Cat-Horse-Itc h*). Suribachi had to be spelled
out in Navajo Code.

A second, larger, flag was raised on Mount Suribachi later that
morning. Joseph Rosenthal, a photographer for Associated Press,
made the climb to the top of the volcano with Rene Gagnon and
the second flag. Six Marines were called to hoist the second flag
as the first was lowered. Rosenthal snapped a photo that would
become the symbol of victory and the valor of the Marine Corps.
One of the men who raised the second flag was Ira Hayes, a Pima
Indian. Rosenthal's photo appeared in newspapers around the
world. The figures in the photo were cast in bronze by sculptor
Felix de Weldon. Today Weldon's bronze statue stands in Arlington

IRA HAYES

Ira Hamilton Hayes, a Pima Indian, was born on January 12, 1923 in Sacaton, Arizona on the Gila River Indian Reservation. Raised in a one-room adobe house, with dirt floors and no indoor plumbing, Ira lived a simple life. His parents, Joe and Nancy Hayes, took him to church, sent him to school, and taught him to honor God and love his flag and country.

In 1942, 19-year-old Ira Hayes enlisted in the U.S. Marine Corps Reserve. After completing basic training in San Diego he went to parachute troopers school and then shipped out to the Pacific theater.

About an hour into the invasion of Iwo Jima, Ira's unit, Easy Company, boarded landing vehicles and headed for shore. By then dead bodies from the preceding waves littered the beach and floated in the water. As Hayes leaped into the shallow water, he saw several men cut down by machine gun fire before they reached the beach.

The men of Easy Company fought their way across Iwo Jima in a bloody four-day battle and joined other troops in surrounding Mount Suribachi. A patrol of 40 men then climbed the 550-foot volcano to secure the highest point on Iwo Jima for U.S. forces. Ira Hayes and the other Marines watched from below, then cheered as a small American flag waved from atop a makeshift pole.

Once Mount Suribachi had been secured, Hayes and three other Marines were selected to run a communication wire to the top of Suribachi. About the same time, Rene Gagnon began to make his way up the mountain with a larger, more visible flag, to replace the first one. Along the way he joined Hayes's patrol. When they reached the top the order was given to lower the small flag and raise the larger one.

Cemetery, a monument to all Marines who have given their lives in defense of their country.

Only three of the six survived Iwo Jima—Ira Hayes, John Bradley, and Rene Gagnon. President Roosevelt honored the three as heros and sent them on a tour to promote war bonds. To many

Joseph Rosenthal, a photographer for Associated Press, and two other photographers arrived just as the second flag was being secured to a pole. Rosenthal planned to frame the lowering and raising of the flags in his photo. However, he was distracted by one of the other photographers. As he glimpsed the movement from the corner of his eye he turned and shot the photo without knowing what he might capture on film. Snapped in that instant, Rosenthal's photo of six battle-weary Marines hoisting the flag became the symbol ofAmerican freedom, patriotism, and spirit. It won Rosenthal a Pulitzer Prize.

As the photo gained national attention, stirring patriotism and boosting morale, President Roosevelt initiated a search for the Marines in the photo. The faces were not visible in the photo so they could only be identified by an eyewitness. Pfc. Rene Gagnon, the Marine who carried the second flag up the mountain, was the first witness to return from Iwo Jima. He was shown an enlarged photo and asked to identify the flag-raisers. He identified five, Henry Hansen, Michael Stank, John Bradley, Franklin Sousley, and himself. Because the sixth man was shy he had asked Gagnon to promise not to reveal his identity. When pressured by government officials Gagnon finally gave in, breaking his promise to Ira Hayes.

Of the six who raised the second flag, only John Bradley, Rene Gagnon and Ira Hayes survived Iwo Jima. President Roosevelt declared the three flag-raisers heroes and sent them on a national tour to promote war bonds. The publicity proved to be too much for Ira Hayes. He was not able to leave behind the horrible memories of war or accept the role of hero. His inability to adjust to civilian life compounded a drinking problem and contributed to his early death. Singer Johnny Cash later wrote a song about Hayes, and his post-war problems took on meaning for many who had trouble readjusting to normal life.

American people these men have become a symbol of all the heroic deeds, recognized and unrecognized, on the bloody battle-fields of World War II.

Code Talker George Soce saw the flag when it first rose over Mount Suribachi. The flag signaled victory, but the island had not been won, only the mountain. He later reported the experience in an interview, "Some were yelling . . . raising their heads. They forgot all about the war. That's when some boys got killed."

General Tadamichi Kuribayashi knew that Iwo Jima would fall to U.S. forces as soon as Mount Suribachi fell. Before the invasion he had instructed his men to fight to the death and kill as many Americans as they could before dying. The few Japanese soldiers who had survived on Suribachi retreated through the tunnels to other parts of the island. Kuribayashi told them to choose a place in the underground fortress that would be their tomb and then fight to the death. In their final moments, these Japanese soldiers made a banzai attack against the U.S. troops on the beach.

The Japanese often made banzai attacks when they faced defeat. According to Japanese tradition, death on the battlefield is far more honorable than surrender. In a banzai attack a Japanese soldier takes whatever weapon and ammunition he has left, often only a sword, and runs, screaming, to attack his enemy. He jumps into a foxhole or charges a machine gun nest with no regard for his own life. He brings honor to himself by killing as many enemy troops as he can before he dies.

Iwo Jima was one of the bloodiest battles in the Pacific. During the 36-day battle, 6,800 U.S. troops sacrificed their lives. Three of them were Code Talkers: Paul Kinlahcheeny, Sam Morgan, and Willie Notah.

Brave men fought the battle for Iwo Jima, many of them going far beyond the call of duty for their country's sake. Twenty-seven Medals of Honor were awarded for extraordinary acts of courage, more than had been awarded in any other battle in the war.

In a speech commending the Marines for the victory on Iwo Jima, Admiral Chester W. Nimitz stated that "Among the Americans who served on Iwo Island, uncommon valor was a common virtue." These words have long been remembered.

Although the Navajo Code remained shrouded in security, the Code Talkers received praise for their skill, speed, and accuracy. Major Howard Connor said, "Were it not for the Navajos, the Marines would never have taken Iwo Jima."

ADMIRAL CHESTER W. NIMITZ

Pacific Fleet/Commander in Chief, Pacific Ocean Areas Admiral Chester W. Nimitz praised the bravery of the men who fought during the 36-day battle for Iwo Jima:

The battle of Iwo Island has been won. The United States Marines by their individual and collective courage have conquered a base which is as necessary to us in our continuing forward movement toward final victory as it was vital to the enemy in staving off ultimate defeat.

By their victory, the 3rd, 4th, and 5th Marine Divisions and other units of the Fifth Amphibious Corps have made an accounting to their country which only history will be able to value fully. Among the Americans who served on Iwo Island, uncommon valor was a common virtue.

The strategic value of the island was quickly proven. On March 4, the first B-29 bomber made an emergency landing on one of the airfields below Mount Suribachi. Repaired and refueled, the massive aircraft took off without incident to complete its mission. By the end of the war, B-29s had made 24,000 emergency landings on Iwo Jima.

Iwo Jima marked a major turning point in the war, opening the gateway to Okinawa. After the island had been secured the 3rd, 4th, and 5th Marine Divisions headed back to Hawaii for more training in preparation for the invasion of mainland Japan. Meanwhile, the 1st, 2nd, and 6th Divisions steamed toward the next island target, Okinawa.

The U.S. forces invaded the large populated island with a massive force on April 1, Easter Sunday, 1945. Although Japan had suffered great losses to its fleet, air force, and army, it continued to fight. The 82-day Okinawa campaign ended July 2, 1945. British observers compared Okinawa to other battles in the Pacific as

... the most audacious and complex enterprise ... yet undertaken by the American Amphibious Forces ... more ships were used, more troops put ashore, more

supplies transported, more bombs dropped, [and] more
naval guns fired against shore targets.

During the whole campaign, U.S. forces relied heavily on the
Navajo net for communications.

Victory came at a high price. Among U.S. troops, about 16,000
were killed or missing in action and almost 53,000 were wounded.
On the Japanese side, about 107,500 were killed in battle and
10,539 surrendered. Facing this massive defeat and the threat of
U.S. invasion of their mainland, the Japanese still refused to
surrender.

In order to avoid a ground invasion and save lives on both sides,
the United States dropped the first atomic bomb on Hiroshima on
August 6, 1945 and a second bomb on Nagasaki three days later.
On August 14, Japan's Emperor Hirohito agreed to an uncondi-
tional surrender.

After the war, the Japanese chief of intelligence, Lieutenant
General Seizo Arisue, admitted that the Japanese deciphered
codes used by the U.S. Army and Army Air Corps but they were
not able to decipher the code used by the Marines. In other words,
they could not crack the Navajo Code.

About 540 Navajos served in the Marines at the end of the war.
Some 375 to 420 of those were trained as Code Talkers while the
rest served in other areas. The end of the war did not signal the
end of the Navajo Code. No one knew when the next conflict
would arise and the unbreakable code remained classified. Instructed to remain silent about their role in the war and the
existence of the code, the Navajos kept the secret until it was
declassified by the U.S. government in 1969.

NOTES

pp. 85–86 "Up to the point . . . " Samuel Eliot Morison, *History of the
United States Naval Operations in World War II, Volume XIV,
Victory in the Pacific* (Boston: Little, Brown and Company,
1960), p. 38.

p. 86   "The *Tennessee* was firing over . . . " Quoted in Kawano, p. 79.

p. 86   "The Iwo Jima sand was . . . " Quoted in Kawano, p. 29.

pp. 87–89 "Iwo Jima is a . . . " Morison, p. 47.

p. 92   "Some were yelling . . . " Interview with George Soce, Doris
          Duke Oral History Collection, ms. 417, Manuscripts Division,
          University of Utah Marriott Library, Salt Lake City, Utah,
          p. 20.

p. 92   "Were it not for the . . . " Quoted in "Navajo Code Talkers,"
          Marine Corps Home Page, http://www.usmc.mil/wwii/
          212a.htm, p. 1.

p. 93   "The battle of Iwo Island . . . " Quoted in http://oberon.hs.
          gettysburg.edu/~pgodinez/iwo.mo.

pp. 93–94 ". . . the most audacious and . . . " Quoted in "Campaign for
          Okinawa," Marine Corps Home page, http://www.usmc.
          mil/wwii/2126.htm, p. 4.

HOME AGAIN

R adio stations flashed news of Japan's surrender across the nation and Americans poured into the streets in jubilant celebration. With the war over, civilians were anxious to welcome the troops home and began making plans for the homecoming.

Although the fighting had ended, U.S. troops maintained their positions in the Pacific and moved to occupy Japan. Some Code Talkers headed home while others remained as part of the postwar force. Assigned to the occupation force in Japan, Paul Blatchford and Rex Malone reported to U.S. Intelligence at Nagasaki. Like the Navajo Code, the atomic bomb was new, having been brought into existence in the effort to defeat Japan. When the bombs were dropped on Hiroshima and Nagasaki, no one knew exactly what would happen. To further their research, army and navy personnel were ordered to prepare reports detailing the aftermath of the bomb in Nagasaki. Scientists back in the States needed this information so they could analyze the power of the atomic bomb. In order to protect security, Blatchford and Malone transmitted these reports in Navajo Code to San Francisco. These men were among the last to transmit messages in Navajo Code in the Pacific. The end of the U.S. occupation of Japan on December 31, 1946, marked the end of the Navajo's "special duty" in World War II.

High-ranking Marine policymakers stamped all information concerning the Navajo Code "confidential." This meant they considered the secrecy of the code vital to the security of the United

States. All documents (letters, memos, and reports) pertaining to the Navajo Code were placed in folders and locked in secure file cabinets. Everyone who knew about the project was ordered to silence on the subject. As a result, the Code Talkers came home much the same way that they left the reservation—under a shroud of secrecy. The existence of the Navajo Code and the Code Talkers would remain a military secret for more than 20 years.

The Code Talkers were ordered never to mention what they did in the war, even to their families. "We were told just to say we were in the war, and that was all right. We weren't looking for glory," said Samuel Billison who served with the 5th Division. During the initial phase of the landing on Iwo Jima, Billison stayed aboard ship to receive messages from the Code Talkers on shore. He was in the third wave that went ashore on the third day. Billison and the other Code Talkers considered the order to keep silent just one more duty to perform for their country. Even without this order, however, those who adhered to traditional beliefs would not have talked about their experiences in the war. The peace-loving Navajo did not want to influence the young with stories of wartime experiences. "Talking about war contaminates the minds of those who should not hear about the bloodshed," explained Code Talker Albert Smith, who served in the Marshall Islands, Saipan, Tinian, and Iwo Jima. "There is always the danger of enticement for the young."

Some people, at least, thought the secrecy surrounding the Navajo Code ended with the war. An article detailing the Navajo Code appeared in the *Honolulu Advertiser* in the summer of 1945. This article written by Ray Coll, Jr., was based on an interview with Lieutenant Colonel J. P. Berkeley, a communications officer with the Fifth Amphibious Marine Corps who had seen the Navajos in action. The article included a detailed account of a Navajo Code Talker transmitting a message. Another article appeared in *The Gallup Independent* dated September 10, 1945. This one, based on an interview with Philip Johnston, detailed Johnston's role in training the Code Talkers. The *San Diego Union* also carried a detailed and lengthy article on September 18, 1945, which described

Navajo Code Talkers "huddled over their radio sets in . . . assault barges, in foxholes, on the beach, in slit trenches deep in the jungle." It went on to reveal that, "The Navajo marines transmitted and received messages, orders, [and] vital information." Although these three newspaper articles described the Code Talker program in detail, the Navajo Code received no further publicity for the next 20 years.

About 3,600 Navajos served in the U.S. military during World War II; of those, about 420 were Code Talkers. In part because of the secrecy and in part because of poor planning, most of the Code Talkers returned from the war with the same number of stripes on their sleeves as they had when they shipped out.

When the original 29 had been recruited into the pilot program, Major James E. Jones and Major General Clayton B. Vogel had seen the Navajos in action and were convinced that a code based on the intricate language would work. Few others, however, shared their enthusiasm. The general thinking had been that when the program failed, the 29 recruits would become general duty Marines. No thought seems to have been given to adding rank for creating the code, completing training, or serving in the capacity of Code Talker.

When the program proved successful, the attention that had been focused on creating the code and training the original 29 shifted to getting the Code Talkers into the Pacific battle zone as soon as possible. They were inducted to meet an emergency need. That emergency grew more severe as the United States continued to lose battles in the Pacific and surrendered the Philippines. Out of necessity, all efforts focused on fighting the war. The small, unique Navajo project, shielded with secrecy, required its own guidelines for promotion and none were written. Johnny R. Manuelito and John A. Benally were promoted to corporal while serving as instructors in the Navajo school. Most Navajo Code Talkers, however, remained at the rank of private first class from the day they completed training until they were discharged.

After the war ended, those who were not involved in the occupation force headed home. Many of the Code Talkers traveled back to the States aboard ships laden with victorious troops. Their special duty ended, the Navajo Code Talkers disappeared into the masses, a few hundred among tens of thousands of returning troops. They returned to ports at San Diego and San Francisco and mustered out of the Marines. After receiving their discharges and severance pay they were on their own. Some headed back to the reservation while others decided to check out city life. A few reenlisted and made a military career for themselves. Wilson Price, for example, retired from the Marines in 1972 after serving 30 years. Another Code Talker, Roy O. Hawthorne, reenlisted with the Army Paratroopers. About 10 years later while in combat duty in Korea, Hawthorne was hit by a mortar shell. As a result of the severe injury, his right leg was amputated. However, Hawthorne stayed in the army two more years. He later explained his reasons for staying in, "It was to me a life that I liked and I wanted to continue there." Hawthorne later returned to the reservation and became a minister.

After receiving their discharges, most of the Code Talkers boarded trains headed east toward their homes and families. As they returned to the reservation, no parades greeted them and no gala parties were held in their honor. The Navajo do not publicly celebrate the homecoming of a person who has done what is expected of him. Such a celebration would be bragging and not acceptable in the culture of the quiet and modest Navajo. As the men came home their people honored them with the respect traditionally given Navajo warriors.

They tried to slip back into the lives they left when they enlisted. Those who had boosted their age to meet Marine requirements went back to class to finish high school. Others, who had finished high school, took advantage of their veteran's benefits to finance a college education.

Following their final orders, they forgot about code talking. As they tried to regain their place in civilian society, they also tried to forget the horrors they had seen and the fears they endured. It was not easy.

Many had purification ceremonies performed for them soon after returning home. The Navajo have long used the three-day Enemyway ceremony of traditional song and dance to help cure an individual who has become ill after going to war.

Some time after George Kirk returned home, he began having nightmares. This is a common problem faced by soldiers of all ethnic backgrounds who have experienced the horrors of combat. For some the nightmares go away after awhile. Others require psychiatric treatment. In Kirk's dreams, Japanese soldiers leaped into his foxhole with him and he revisited the fears he had experienced on the battlefield. His wife persuaded him to go to a medicine man. The medicine man performed the traditional Enemyway ceremony believed to slay the enemy presence. Kirk's nightmares of the war disappeared following the ceremony.

Roy Notah enlisted when he was 20 and served four years in combat from Guadalcanal to Okinawa. Twenty years after the war, his battlefield experiences began to haunt him. In vivid hallucinations his Marine insignia turned into a Japanese dragon. He heard the voice of the dragon threaten him with return to the war zone. "It seemed so real . . . The dragon tells me, he was going to take me back to the Pacific and make statue out of me." His wife, Louise, took him to a traditional Navajo medicine man for prayer. Roy did not experience any more hallucinations after he received the traditional medicine.

Other Navajos did not have the ceremony performed for them because they were either raised Christian or they no longer believed in the traditional medicine after being away from the reservation. Others were so poor they couldn't afford the services of a medicine man. Sometimes the medicine man offered his services free to those who couldn't pay, and other times the ailing person obtained relief by attending tribal dances.

Bound by tradition and patriotism, the Code Talkers kept their silence until the U.S. government declassified the Navajo Code in 1969. By this time computer technology, with the ability to create extremely complex codes, rendered the Navajo Code obsolete. Twenty-three years after the war ended, the secret could be told.

The released documents revealed the progress of the Navajo project from Johnston's presentation of the idea, to authorization to enlist the original 29, to deployment in the Pacific and included words of praise from commanding officers at the front. The details of the Code Talkers in action, however, were known only to a few hundred Navajo Marines and many of them had died by the time their story could be told.

The first public recognition finally came during the annual reunion of the 4th Marine Division held in Chicago in 1969. Every year the 4th Division gave special honor to a member at the reunion. This honor usually went to a recipient of the Medal of Honor or a high-ranking officer who had served in the 4th Division. Lee Cannon served on the honors committee for the 1969 reunion. He had knowledge of the Code Talkers and suggested that these veterans who had never received any recognition be given the honor.

The committee spent many months preparing for the event. Individual Navajo Code Talkers were found and invited. Arrangements were made for their transportation and stay in Chicago. In addition, great care was given in selecting a design for a special medallion that would be presented to the Code Talkers. Inspiration for the design came from a painting of Ira Hayes by Joe Ruiz Grandee. Grandee's painting features Ira Hayes in full Pima hunting regalia riding an Indian pony with the image of the second flag raising on Iwo Jima in the background. The engraved medallions hung from leather thongs threaded through red, white, and blue beads.

Twenty Code Talkers attended the reunion, fifteen who served in the 4th Division plus one who had served in each of the other five Divisions. In the two days preceding the reunion ceremonies, the Code Talkers were given a sightseeing tour of the city and treated to a pow wow hosted by the Indians of Chicago at the American Indian Center. June 28, the day of the reunion, began as the Code Talkers joined the other Marines in a parade through downtown Chicago, which ended with a memorial service at Pioneer Court. At the banquet that night, each Code Talker was called forward and presented one of the specially designed medallions. These medallions honored the Code Talkers for their "Meritorious Service in Communications," a long overdue acknowledgment of their contribution to America. The Code Talkers themselves had not realized the significance of their service until this time. They had done what they were asked to do. They had created an unbreakable combat code based on their language. They used the code to transmit and receive vital information in some of the heaviest and bloodiest combat America had ever seen.

During the Reunion at Window Rock, Arizona in 1971, Code Talkers Jim Cody, Jimmie King, and Dean Wilson transmit a message over a field radio for old times' sake. *(Special Collections, University of Utah Photo #NT-255)*

And, they followed orders to remain silent about their role in the war. American and Indian, the medallion bridged two worlds as the Code Talkers were finally recognized for patriotism at its best.

Valuable as their contribution was, the Code Talkers were only one part of America's fighting force. Code Talker Kee Etsicity explained the Code Talkers' role this way, "The Marine Corps is like a wheel with many different spokes. The code talkers were one spoke in the Marine Corps wheel, an important one, but contained within the whole."

In July 1971 the U.S. Marine Corps and the Navajo Tribe co-sponsored a two-day Code Talker reunion at Window Rock, Arizona. Interviewers from the Doris Duke Oral History Project at the University of Utah and representatives of the Marine Corps interviewed the Code Talkers. Encouraged to tell their stories at last, some of them gave long detailed accounts of their experiences. Others, however, remained reluctant to break the silence and simply answered the questions of the interviewer. Through these accounts the world can know what the Code Talkers did. It was much more than relaying messages in their native language. Human code machines, they instantly translated written English to oral code and spoke in code to a distant partner, who translated the coded message back into written English. These messages, vital and urgent, made the difference in the outcome of many battles. If radio or phone equipment failed, the Code Talker carried the message on foot. As runners they made their way across sandy beaches, through jungles, or up steep rocky slopes from one outpost position to another. During this extremely dangerous mission, runners avoided bursting mortar shells and slipped past sharp-eyed snipers.

As they told their stories, the picture became clear. Under the severest combat conditions, the Navajos possessed the extraordinary skills that would get the messages through. Unrecognized for almost a quarter of a century, these men were heroes who saved many lives.

Most Navajo Code Talkers were assigned to advancing rifle companies and were among the first to go ashore during a

THE DORIS DUKE COLLECTION

In 1925, 13-year-old Doris Duke inherited $100 million in assets from her father, James Buchanan "Buck" Duke, founder of the American Tobacco Company.
Doris grew up to be a good businesswoman. By the time she died at age 80, her estate was valued at more than a billion dollars. Although she lived an extravagant lifestyle, her smart investments in real estate, art, and business allowed her to set up several million-dollar charitable trusts. Through one of these trusts, Doris Duke supported the North American Indian Oral History Project at the University of Utah. In 1971 interviewers from the university recorded approximately 60 hours of interviews with the Navajo Code Talkers at their reunion. These tapes were then transcribed and bound to become a part of the University's Special Collections.

landing. When U.S. Marines landed on Okinawa, Harry Benally was in one of the first waves. During the landing, between sending coded messages, Benally captured and disarmed 14 Japanese soldiers. "You did what you had to do," he later told a *Los Angeles Times* reporter.

During the reunion, the 69 Code Talkers present organized the Code Talker Association and elected officers. John Benally headed the organization as chairman. James Nahkai took the position of vice-chairman, and William McCabe became secretary-treasurer. Benally and McCabe were among the original 29 Code Talkers, and Nahkai served in the Pacific from the Solomon Islands to Okinawa and later in China. The Code Talker Association is dedicated to educating the Navajo people and general public about the role the Code Talkers played during World War II.

In December 1971, President Richard Nixon presented the Navajo Code Talkers with a certificate of appreciation on behalf of the nation. He thanked them for their "patriotism, resourcefulness, and courage."

Dressed in the Association uniform, Code Talkers from the 3rd and 4th Marine Divisions posed for this group photo during a commemoration of the landing on Iwo Jima. *(Photo courtesy Defense Visual Information Center (DVIC), March AFB, #DM-SC-88-07318)*

After the creation of the Association, the Code Talkers adopted a specially designed logo, flag, and uniform. A mix of Marine Corps and Navajo culture, the original uniform consisted of a turquoise cap, gold velveteen shirt, and khaki trousers. They later switched to a red cap. In 1973 members of the Association began marching in Veteran's Day parades throughout the Southwest. They also visited schools on and off the reservation, talking to students about their service in World War II. As word spread about the Navajo Code Talkers they became a source of pride for the Navajo Nation.

Opportunities soon came for national appearances. Navajo Code Talkers marched in the Tournament of Roses parade in Pasadena, California on New Years Day, 1975. Two years later, newly elected president Jimmy Carter invited the Code Talkers to march in his inauguration parade on January 20, 1977. That same year, as America celebrated her bicentennial, a Code Talkers color guard marched ahead of the 350-member All-Arizona Marching Band in parades in Washington, D.C. and Philadelphia.

The Code Talkers enjoyed the travel and the parades brought recognition and glory. The Marine Corps acknowledged the Code Talker's contribution in the Pacific by recruiting an all-Navajo platoon in observance of the 39th anniversary of the original 29. Many of the young men in this platoon were relatives of the Code Talkers.

In 1982, Congress passed a resolution that designated August 14, 1982 as National Navajo Code Talkers Day. The date coincided with the 37th anniversary of the Japanese surrender, or V-J (Victory in Japan) Day. On behalf of Congress, President Ronald Reagan issued a proclamation asking the American people to join him in a tribute to "all members of the Navajo Nation and to all Native Americans who gave their special talents and their lives so that others might live."

In 1992, Keith Little was invited to Washington, D.C. to participate in the dedication of a Code Talker exhibit in the Pentagon. During the ceremony Little received and translated a prayer for peace telephoned to him by a Code Talker in Arizona.

Many years after the war, an all Navajo platoon was recruited in honor of the original 29. Members of that platoon, pictured here, take up defensive positions during combat field training in 1982. *(Photo courtesy Defense Visual Information Center (DVIC), March AFB, #DM-SN-82-03217)*

In the years that followed the declassification of the Navajo Code, the Code Talkers have been honored at many Veteran's Day celebrations. In November 1995, a bust of Code Talker Carl Gorman sculpted by his son, noted artist R. C. Gorman, was unveiled at the University of Northern Arizona. The four-foot bronze bust of Gorman rests on an eight-foot sandstone pedestal. The names of the original 29 are engraved on a plaque anchored to the pedestal. The statue was a gift from R. C. Gorman to his alma mater and a tribute to the Navajo Code Talkers. Marine Colonel Willis Hansen, representing the Marine Corps at the ceremony, called the sculpture "a long overdue monument to the dedication and bravery of a unique group of Americans."

In March 1995, Thomas Begay returned to Iwo Jima. One of almost 900 Americans, he walked on the black sand beaches in commemoration of the 50th anniversary of the battle. Begay climbed Mount Suribachi and shouted the code for I-W-O J-I-M-A.

His wife, Nina, stood nearby chanting "Iwo, Iwo, Iwo," keeping rhythm with the small drum she carried. Her chants, wafting over the black sands below, called to the spirits of Americans who died there.

Americans were not alone in remembering those who lost their lives on Iwo Jima. About 100 Japanese came to the island that day. Among them was a frail woman, dressed in black, the widow of Lieutenant General Tadamichi Kuribayashi. With the United States and Japan no longer enemies, Yoshi Kuribayashi, well into her nineties, spoke in Japanese about the emotional price both countries paid in the war. Her words have been translated into English:

> Japanese and Americans bravely fought for their own nations and their fellow soldiers . . . every soldier was admired as a hero. When I think about their spirits, I cannot help but shed tears.

NOTES

p. 97   "We were told just . . . " Quoted in Tony Perry, "Words of Praise for Navajo Code Talkers' Heroics," *Los Angeles Times,* November 12, 1995 (Electric Library download, p. 2).

p. 97   "Talking about war . . . " Quoted in Watson, p. 42.

p. 98   "huddled over their radio . . . " "Navajo 'Hidden' Language Makes Unbreakable U.S. Code," *San Diego Union,* September 18, 1945.

p. 99   "It was to me . . . ." Hawthorne, interview, Doris Duke Oral History Collection, p. 9.

p. 100   "It seemed so real . . . " Quoted in Markey Shebala, "Sharing War," *News from Indian Country,* December 12, 1995 (Electronic Library download, p. 2).

p. 103   "The Marine Corps is . . . " Quoted in McClain, p. 229.

p. 104   "You did what you . . . " Quoted in Perry, p. 2.

p. 104   "Patriotism, resourcefulness . . . " Quoted in William R. Wilson, "Code Talkers," *American History* 37, no. 6 (February 1997), p. 67.

p. 106   "all members of the Navajo . . . " Quoted in McClain, pp. 235–236.

p. 107   "a long overdue monument . . . " Quoted in Perry, p. 1.

p. 108   "Japanese and Americans bravely . . . " Quoted in Susan Kreifels, "Walking the Sands and Weeping," *Navy Times,* March 27, 1995, p. 20.

THE CODE
TALKERS'
CONTRIBUTION

B y 1997 the number of surviving Code Talkers had dwin-
dled to "around 200 with 50 to 60 active in the association,"
according to Albert Smith, president of the Code Talker Association. Still honored in Veterans' Day parades, they ride more often
than walk. Eight hearty Code Talkers—Albert Smith, Samuel
Billison, Keith Little, Jimmy Begay, Samuel Smith, Samuel Tso,
Wilfred Billey, and Alfred Peaches—marched in President Clin-
ton's second inaugural parade.

Recognized in presidential parades and recorded in American
history, the Code Talkers' contribution established a legacy for the
Navajo Nation that will be handed down through future generations. An oppressed people who had vowed never to forget the
suffering of the Long Walk now had national heroes to remember.
The Code Talkers changed the attitude toward the Navajo culture
for the Navajo as well as the non-Navajo. Today Navajo children
learn about the Code Talkers in school and take pride in their
native tongue and heritage.

Recruited in 1942, these young Navajo men boldly left the
reservation to venture into the unknown. Asked to use their native
language to benefit national security, they maintained their
Navajo identity in the Marine Corps. No one objected that those

who held to traditional values carried pouches of sacred corn pollen tied at their waists. The Navajo ritual they performed during prayers at dawn drew little attention. In combat zones, from Guadalcanal to Okinawa, they held small ceremonies among themselves, before each landing. They were Navajo; they were American. They practiced their religion.

Called from the reservation to contribute a portion of their culture, they joined America's fiercest fighting team. For the first time, they found that they could walk within the realms of both cultures. Once they donned the uniform, they were Marines, men in a fighting unit, facing a common enemy. In the confines of a foxhole, skin color tended to lose its significance. Men in combat soon learned respect for radiomen who spoke a language the enemy could not understand, in a code no one except a Navajo Code Talker could decipher. The success of the unbreakable code brought respect from their comrades and kindled pride in the Code Talkers.

As they returned home and packed their Marine uniforms away, they discovered civilian life on the reservation had not changed. They were Indians again. Some were content to slip back into the life they had left tending their corn fields and sheep. Some of them took jobs with the BIA and stayed on the reservation. These jobs included construction and repair of BIA facilities and janitorial and lunchroom positions at BIA schools. There were also a few interpreter positions in Health Service. Of the many return-ing veterans, the BIA could employ only a few of those who did not further their education. As a result, many veterans left the reservation to seek jobs in the cities.

Those who left established their families in urban America. Their children grew up away from the extended Navajo families and under the influence of white America. They lost touch with their Indian heritage, its tradition and culture.

Teddy Draper's experience at the end of the war helped him realize the need for these children to have an opportunity to study their native language. During the war, Draper learned to speak Japanese. Later, he served as an interpreter during the U.S.

occupation of Japan. As he observed the defeated Japanese in their struggle to regain balance in their lives, he realized the importance of native language. This stirred memories of his boarding school days when he was punished for speaking the Navajo language. Draper wanted to make sure the language would not be lost. He made a pledge to himself that if he made it back to the reservation safely, he would "become a Navajo language teacher and educate young Navajos." During his military and Code Talker training, Draper picked up teaching techniques and an appreciation for education. He later used this knowledge to keep the pledge he made to himself by teaching the Navajo language to Navajo children.

Others also went to college on the GI Bill and returned to the reservation as teachers. With a rekindled pride in their culture they began to merge traditional teachings with modern knowledge. Today, the Navajo Community College, with campuses located throughout the reservation at Tsaile, Chinle, Tuba City, Ganado, Window Rock, Shiprock, and Crownpoint, incorporates tribal values and beliefs into all academic programs. The Navajo Philosophy of Learning follows the traditional Navajo organization of knowledge and approach to problem solving—the cycles of nature and the four cardinal directions. For example, according to the American Indian College Fund's 1993 Annual Report:

> The instructor, while covering everything required in . . .
> a college biology course may also teach the Navajo
> classification systems of plants and animals. Other disci-
> plines, such as chemistry, physics, sociology and spiritu-
> ality, may be drawn in to demonstrate interrelationships
> in the natural world. The instructor may explain the
> male and female principles of nature, as understood by
> the Navajo, and adopt a traditional, cyclical pattern of
> presenting the information.

The overall education includes traditional wisdom such as: understanding of one's relationship with nature, respect for elders, getting along with others, and living a balanced, healthy life. Students frequently meet with Navajo spiritual leaders and medi-

CARL GORMAN

Thirty-five-years old and too old for the Marines, Carl Gorman lied about his age to enlist for "special service." One of the original 29, Gorman helped create the Navajo Code and served in the Pacific from Guadalcanal to Saipan. He fell victim to malaria in the mosquito infested Pacific and was evacuated from Saipan. He spent the rest of his military career in hospitals recuperating from the tropical disease.

After receiving his honorable discharge in winter of 1945 he used his veteran's benefits to study art at Otis Institute. He became a successful artist and teacher. While living in Los Angeles, California, he served as leader of the urban Navajo community there. During this time Carl's son, R. C. Gorman, was gaining recognition as an artist. The two held father-son exhibits. R. C. became a world-famous artist and later sculpted a bust of his father, which he donated to the University of Northern Arizona in honor of the Code Talkers. Carl Gorman returned to the reservation where he accepted a position as director of the Navajo Arts and Crafts Guild. He later served as president of the Code Talker Association. In January 1998 he died. Through the years he was often seen on Veterans' Day in the Code Talker uniform, marching in parades. As a spokesman, Gorman helped educate Navajo and all Americans about the Code Talker role in World War II. He was an excellent role model and a respected leader among the Navajo.

cine men who incorporate these traditional values in higher education.

Some of the Code Talkers used their GI Bill to study art. Those who gained recognition in the art world brought attention to tribal arts and crafts including Navajo sand paintings, pottery, and rugs. Code Talker Carl Gorman studied art at Otis Art Institute in Los Angeles, California. After four years his GI Bill ran out, and he took a position as a technical illustrator at Douglas Aircraft in Santa Monica. With this job he was able to pay his own way at the Ottis Institute and continue studying art in the evenings. While gaining recognition for his artistic talents he became a leader among the urban Navajo. He later moved back to the reservation where he directed the Navajo Arts and Crafts Guild. Today, Navajo are well known for their arts and crafts. Marketing these products is one of the more profitable businesses on the reservation.

Recognized as national heroes, the Code Talkers stirred the imagination of Hollywood. In 1996, a popular television program, *X-Files*, used a Code Talker plot in one of their weekly science fiction thrillers. A few months later, on January 31, 1997, Dan Rather's CBS Evening News turned its attention toward the Code Talkers in the "Travels with Harry" segment. Harry Smith visited the Navajo reservation, and Dan Rather interviewed Carl Gorman at his home. The national audience saw clips of the Navajo Code Talkers in action during World War II and the unveiling of the bust of Gorman at the University of Northern Arizona. In tribute to the Code Talkers' contribution in World War II, Dan Rather said, "Without them the American way of life might not have survived." Ninety-year-old Gorman, however, showed the true heart of a Marine with his closing statement, "Old Marines never die, they just go to hell and regroup."

The story of these Navajo Marines will be passed down to future generations. However, the knowledge is no longer preserved only in the memories of the Navajo elders. These events are recorded in American history and stored in the National Archives. There's a monument in the National Cemetery and an exhibit at the National Cryptologic Museum at the National Security Agency. They waited a long time but America has finally raised its hand in salute to these Navajo Marines.

NOTES

p. 110   "around 200 with 50 . . . " Albert Smith, interview by Deanne Durrett, March 1997.

p. 112   "become a Navajo language . . . " Quoted in Wilson, p. 66.

p. 112   "The instructor, while . . . " "Tribal Values and Beliefs: Ensuring a Diversity of World Views," 1993 Annual Report, American Indian College Fund, http://hanksville.phast.umass.edu/ defs/independent/AICF/values.html.

SELECTED
FURTHER READING LIST

BOOKS ABOUT THE CODE TALKERS

Aaseng, Nathan. *Navajo Code Talkers*. New York: Walker, 1992. A young adult book on the Code Talkers covering their role in World War II.

Greenberg, Henry, and Georgia Greenberg. *Power of a Navajo, Carl Gorman: The Man and His Life*. Santa Fe, New Mexico: Clear Light Publishers, 1996. This biography covers Carl Gorman's life including his Code Talker experience and art career. It is an adult book but not too difficult.

Jones, Catherine. *Navajo Code Talkers: Native American Heroes*. San Diego, Calif.: Tudor Publishing Company, 1998. A short 31-page book for young readers on the Code Talkers.

Kawano, Kenji. *Warriors: Navajo Code Talkers*. Flagstaff, Arizona: Northland Publishing Co., 1990. A book of photos, many taken by Kawano many years after the war ended, accompanied by quotes from the Navajo Code Talkers. The introduction gives an account of the Code Talkers during the war.

McClain, S. *Navajo Weapon*. Boulder, Colorado: Books Beyond Borders, Inc., 1994. An in-depth look at the Navajo Code Talkers, their role in World War II, and civilian life after the war. This book is adult reading level but not too difficult.

Paul, Doris A. *The Navajo Code Talkers*. Philadelphia: Dorrance & Company, 1973. An account of the Navajo Code Talkers and their role in World War II and civilian life up to the early 1970s.

BOOKS ABOUT WORLD WAR II

Black, Wallace B., and Jean F. Blashfield. *Guadalcanal*. New York: Crestwood House, 1992. This book is an easy-to-read account of the battle on Guadalcanal during World War II.

———. *Island Hopping in the Pacific*. New York: Crestwood House, 1993. This book is an easy-to-read overview of the U.S. Island Hopping Campaign from Guadalcanal to Okinawa.

———. *Iwo Jima and Okinawa*. New York: Crestwood House, 1993. This book is an easy-to-read account of the battles between the United States and Japan on the islands of Iwo Jima and Okinawa during World War II.

Devaney, John. *America Goes to War: 1941*. New York: Walker and Company, 1991.

———. *America Fights the Tide: 1942*. New York: Walker and Company, 1992.

———. *America on the Attack: 1943*. New York: Walker and Company, 1993.

———. *America Storms the Beaches: 1944*. New York: Walker and Company, 1994.

———. *America Triumphs: 1945*. New York: Walker and Company, 1995. In this five-book series Devaney gives a day-by-day account of the war on the battlefronts throughout Europe and the Pacific as well as the homefront in America. The you-are-there type vignettes cover the war from all angles. For young readers.

Nardo, Don. *World War II: The War in the Pacific*. San Diego: Lucent Books, 1991. This young adult book is an overview of the war in the Pacific from beginning to end, including America's prewar relationship with Japan, Japan's motivation to fight to the bitter end, details of the battles on the Pacific islands, and the dropping of the atomic bomb.

Rice, Earle, Jr. *The Attack on Pearl Harbor*. San Diego: Lucent Books, 1996. A young adult account of the attack on Pearl Harbor and America's entry into World War II.

BOOKS ABOUT THE NAVAJO

Bingham, Sam, and Janet Bingham. *Between Sacred Mountains: Navajo Stories and Lessons from the Land*. Tucson, Arizona: Sun Tracks/University of Arizona Press, reprint 1984. (Originally published: Chinle, Arizona: Rock Point Community School, 1982.) A excellent book about Navajo by Navajo for Navajo, full of first person accounts about the land between the Sacred Mountains, Navajo life and culture.

Iverson, Peter. *Navajos*. New York: Chelsea House, 1990. This young adult book includes a look at the history, culture, changing fortunes, and current situation of the Navajo.

New Mexico People & Energy Collective. *Red Ribbons for Emma*. Berkeley: New Seed Press, 1981. This brief biography offers a glimpse into a Navajo sheepherder's daily life, her love of the land, and struggle to protect the environment.

Trahant, Lenora Begay. *The Success of the Navajo Arts and Crafts Enterprise*. New York: Walker and Company, 1996. A young adult history of this successful Navajo business network that links jewelers and weavers with a staff of bookkeepers, marketers, and suppliers to help the Navajo artisans make a living at their craft.

Wood, Leigh Hope. *The Navajo Indians*. New York: Chelsea House, 1991. An easy-to-read book that examines the history, culture, and future prospects of the Navajo.

INDEX

Italic page numbers indicate illustrations.
Boldface page numbers indicate main topics.
Page numbers followed by *m* indicate maps.

A

Adam, Lucy W. 23
Akee, Dan 66
alphabet
    Navajo Code 38, 40, **41**
    words to distinguish letters of 39–40
American Indian College Fund 112
Apache, Mescalero 5
Arisue, Seizo 94
Arizona, statehood 7
Arizona, U.S.S. 14, 15
Arizona Highways 54–55
Arlington National Cemetery 89–90, 114
Army, U.S., 36th Division, 142nd Infantry 9–11
atomic bomb 94
    analysis of effect of 96

B

Bahe Jr., Henry *53*
Bailey, Richard P. 62
Bataan Death March 78
Begay, Charlie 63, 68
Begay, Jimmy 110
Begay, Samuel 63
Begay, Thomas H. 86, 107–108
Benally, Harry 104
Benally, John A. 39, *39*, 50, 55, 98
    Code Talker Association and 104
Berkeley, J. P. 97
Billey, Wilfred 110
Billiman, Howard *39*, 56
Billison, Albert 110
Billison, Samuel 97
Billy, Albert 10
Bitsie, Wilsie 32–33, 39, 40, 63, 68

Blatchford, Paul 66, 96
Blessingway Ceremony 29, **30**
Bloor, A. W. 10–11
Bobb, Mitchell 9–10
Bonham, Richard 77
Bosque Redondo 5
    young Navajo woman at *6*
Bradley, John 90, 91
Brown, Cosey 27–28, 63
Brown, Victor 10
Bureau of Indian Affairs (BIA) 23, 26, 27
Busihido philosophy 62

C

Camp Elliott 35, 36, 37–38, *37*, 53–54
Cannon, Lee 100–101
Cape Torokina 79
Carlson, Evans F. 68
Carlson, Raymond 54
Carlson's Raiders 68–69
Carson, Kit 4
Carterby, Ben 10
Cash, Johnny 91
Cavalry, U.S. 4
    scorched earth policy 4–5
CBS Evening News 114
Chee, John 63
Choctaw Indians 9–12
    wartime communications by 10–11
Code Talker Association 104, *105*
    appearances of 106
    1997 members of 110
code talkers *See also* comunications, combat;
    Navajo Code Talkers
    Indian tribes recognized as 18
    origins of army use 9–10

Cody, Jim 102
Coll Jr., Ray 97
communications, combat 8, 18
    Choctaw Indians in WWI 10–11
    Indian languages as 19
    military codes 37
    World War I, code talkers 11–12
Connor, Howard 86–87, 92
Crawford, Eugene 30, 31, 63, 68
    mistaken for Japanese 77
    on security at Camp Elliott 36
Curley, David 63
Currin, Lieutenant Colonel 68

D

Daiker, Fred H. 23
Dale, Ray 53
Dergance, Robert M. 55
Dine 1
Dodge, Chee 27
Doris Duke Collection **104**
Doris Duke Oral History Project 103, 104
Draper, Teddy 111–112
Duffy, Sergeant 33

E

Easy Company, 5th Division, 28th Marines 88,
    89, 90
Edson, Merritt A. 68
Edson, U.S.S. 68
Edwards, James (Jimpson M.) 10
Enemyway ceremony 100
Etsicity, Kee 103

F

Fort Defiance 29
Foster, Harold 67, 75
4th Division, Marine Corps 101
Frazier, Tobias 11
Fuchida, Mitsuo 13

G

Gagnon, Rene 89, 90
Gallup Independent, The 97
German communication interceptions 9
    Choctaw code talkers and 11–12
    research of Indian languages 12
Gorman, Carl 27, 43, **113**
    bust of 107
    contributions of 113–114
Gorman, Howard 17
Gorman, R. C. 106, 113
Grandee, Joe Ruiz 101
Guadalcanal **59–69**, 61*m*
    importance of airfield on 59
    Japanese abandon 69
    as staging area 72
    strategic importance of **62**
Guam 79

H

Hall, George T. 29, 34
Hampton, Benjamin W. 11
Hansen, Henry 91
Hansen, Willis 107
Haskie, Ross 43, 63
Hawthorne, Roy O. 71, 99
Hayes, Ira 89, **90**, 91
    painting of, for Code Talkers medal 101
Henderson Field, Guadalcanal 63
Holcomb, Thomas 22, 26, 56
Honolulu Advisor 97
Housewood, Johnson 80
Howard, A. F. 74
Hunt, Lieutenant 63–64

I

Ilthma, Oscar 39–40
Ironbottom Sound 61
Iwo Jima 1–2, *2*, 83*m*
    description 84
    difficult assault of 87–89
    Easy Company raising flag on *88*
    50th anniversary of taking of 107–108
    final Japanese assault on 92
    flag raising photo 89, 90
    Marines landing on 85–86
    Navajo Code Talkers operations on 86–87
    strategic importance of 82–83, 93–94
    Thomas Begay returns to 107–108

J

Japanese
    aggression against U.S. 17, 61–62
    at Iwo Jima 1–2
    Pearl Harbor mission 13–15, 15*m*
Johnston, Philip 19–21, *49*, 54, 55, 97
    recruiting Navajo Code Talkers 21, 48–49
Jones, James E. 19–21, 22, 98

K

Kassanaviod, Forrest 18–19
Keedah Sr., Wilson 16
Kennepah, Jesse 29
Kieyoomia, Joe **78**
King, Jimmie 53, 80, 81, *102*
    on classified messages 74–75
    high standards of 56–57
Kinlahcheeny, Paul 92
Kirk, George 80, 100
Kluckhohn, Clyde 5
Kontz, Rex *39*, 56
Kuribayashi, Tadamichi 84, 92
Kuribayashi, Yoshi 108

L

Lawrence, Captain 9
Leighton, Dorothea 5
Leonard, Alfred 63
Little, Keith 16, 106, 110
Liversedge, Harry B. 68
Lockard, G. R. 65
long-distance communication 8
Long Walk 3*m*, 5, 8
Louis, Solomon Bond 9–10

M

Malone, Rex 96
Manuelito, Johnny R. 39, 49, 50, 55, 98
Marine Corps, U.S. 1
  382nd (Navajo) Platoon 33
  age requirements for 27
  all Navajo platoon 106, 107
  begin Guadalcanal assault 60, 62–63
  Code Talkers reunion 101–102, 103
  demerit system 32
  distribution of Navajo Code Talkers in field
  74
  Iwo Jima landing 85–86, 85
  Navajo beliefs and 65–67, 110–111
  weight requirements for 28
Marine Hymn, Navajo version 51, **52**
Masterkey, The 19
Maytubby, Pete 11
McCabe, William 39, 63, 79, 80
  Code Talker Association and 104
  on memorizing the code 43
  on Navajo code vs. code machine 64
  on Navajo translation capabilities 45
McCaskill, J. C. 23
Mikawa, Gunichi 60–61
  resemblance to Navajo 75
Morgan, J. C. 17
Morgan, Ralph 79
Morgan, Sam 92
Mount Suribachi 88, 89, 90, 91–92
Myer, Albert J. 8

N

Nakai, James 104
National Archives 114
National Cemetery *See* Arlington National
  Cemetery
National Cryptologic Museum 18, 114
National Navajo Code Talkers Day 106
Navajo **1–12**
  beliefs, Marine Corps and 65–67, 110–111
  Blessingway ceremony 29, **30**
  clans 4
  code based on language of 19–21
  on contamination of war 97
  desert knowledge 34
  Enemyway ceremony 100
  enlisting for World War II 16
  horse herds 3

as Japanese prisoner-of-war 78
  lands 3*m*
  Long Walk to Bosque Redondo 5
  Philosophy of Learning 112–113
  pride in Code Talkers legacy 110
  tested for combat communication 22
  Tribal Council, Window Rock resolution **17**
Navajo, The (Kluckhohn and Leighton) 5
Navajo code
  alphabet 38, 40, **41**
  versus code machine 64
  confidentiality of 96–97
  cryptologist evaluation of 50–51
  declassification of 100–101
  importance to Iwo Jima assault 84
  Japanese inability to break 94
  military terms creation 38, 41–43
  months of the year **44**
  in operation **71–81**
  protection of 77
  school at Camp Elliott 50–52
  on trial on Guadalcanal 63–64
  U.S. intelligence attempts to break 45
Navajo Code Talkers **1–2**
  arrive on Guadalcanal 63
  bodyguards for 77
  boot camp experiences 30–35
  Camp Elliott ceremonial dance 51–52, 53
  Chicago reunion and honor for 101–103
  code field trials 44
  combat experiences 79–81
  contribution of 103–104, 110–114
  distribution in field **74**
  Enemyway ceremony for 100
  on enlisting in the military 16
  homecoming 99, 111
  honored by 4th Division, Marine Corps
    101–102
  induction into Marine Corps 30
  instructors for 39, 40
  Iwo Jima operations 86–87
  in jungle combat 64–67
  Marine Corps recruitment requirements
    and 27–28
  Marines distrust of 73–75
  original 29 **33**
  physical resemblance to Japanese 75–77
  pilot project authorized 23
  praise for Iwo Jima work 92
  promotions overlooked for 98
  publicity about 52–53, 54–55, 97–98
  recruiting original 29 25–35
  relay that Mount Suribachi taken 89
  from reservation to Marine Corps 28*m*
  using battery-powered radios 67
  using walkie-talkie 64
  Window Rock reunion 103
Navajo language **20**
  development as communication code 19–21
  teaching 112
Navajo Reservation 6–7
Navajo Stock Reduction Program 7–8
Nelson, Jeff 11
New Mexico, statehood 7
Nez, Chester 63

Nimitz, Chester W. 92, **93**
Nixon, Richard 104
Noble, A. H. 46
Notah, Roy 100
Notah, Willie 92

O

O'Hugh, Frank 60–61
Oklahoma 14, 15
Oklahombi, Joseph 10
Oliver, Lloyd 63

P

Peachers, Alfred 110
Pearl Harbor, Japanese attack of 13–14, *14*, 15*m*
Peleliu 79, 80
Price, Wilson 43, 99

R

radios
    TBX, battery-powered *67*
    types used in combat 75
Raiders Battalion 68–69
Rather, Dan 114
Reagan, Ronald 106
Roosevelt, Franklin D. 7, 16, 90
Roosevelt, James 68
Rosenthal, Joseph 89, **91**

S

San Diego Union 97–98
Sandoval, Merril L. 86
Sandoval, Peter 87
Schrier, Harold G. 89
Shannon, Frank 55
Shinn, Frank 27
Signal Corps, U.S. Army 8
Singer, Tom 80
Smith, Albert 97, 110
Smith, Harry 114
Smith, Samuel 110
Soce, George 91–92
Sousley, Franklin 91
Stank, Michael 91
Stewart, James M. 54, 55
Stillwell, Captain 50–51

T

Taylor, Robert 11
Thirty Days Behind the Lines operation 69
382nd (Navajo) Platoon, Marine Corps 33
    asking for help 43
    assigned to create the code 37–39
    boot camp *31*, 32–35

creating the code 39–43
memorizing the code 43
practice coding 43–44
praise for 46
Signal Corps training 45
Tokyo Rose 79
Toledo, Bill 77
Toledo, Frank 72
Toledo, Preston 72
Tracy, Peter *39*, 56
Treaty of 1868 6
Treaty of Guadalupe Hidalgo 3
Trent, Dover P. 54
Tribal Council, Navajo
    on Selective Service recruiting 26
Tso, Samuel 110
Tsosie, Harry 79
Tulagi, Japanese occupy 59
Turnage, A. H. 23

U

Underhill, James L. 34–35

V

Vandergrift, Alexander A. 63
Veach, Walter 10
Vogel, Clayton B. 21–22, 98
    recruiting Navajos 26–27
    transfer to New Zealand 60

W

Weldon, Felix de 89–90
Williams, Alex 29
Wilson, Calvin 11
Wilson, Dean *102*
Wilson, William Dean 27
Woodworth, Wethered 23, 26
World War I
    Choctaw Indians communications 9–12,
        10–11
    Comanche Indians communications 12
World War II
    combat communication needs 19
    Pacific campaign 93–94
Wright, Mike 9–10

X

X-Files 114

Y

Yazzie, Felix 43, 63, 68
Yazzie, Pahe D. 16
Yazzie, William 75
Yellow, Charlie 7